F. R. Wegg-Prosser

Galileo & His judges

F. R. Wegg-Prosser

Galileo & His judges

ISBN/EAN: 9783337735579

Printed in Europe, USA, Canada, Australia, Japan

Cover: Foto ©ninafisch / pixelio.de

More available books at **www.hansebooks.com**

GALILEO AND HIS JUDGES

BY

F. R. WEGG-PROSSER.

LONDON: CHAPMAN AND HALL,
Limited.
1889.

PREFACE.

THERE is no name in the annals of science which has been the occasion of so long and fierce a controversy as that of Galileo. The historian, the astronomer, and the theologian have all had a share in it. Sometimes there has been a pause in the strife, and the question has been allowed to rest; but after a while another disputant has rekindled the embers, and the struggle has recommenced. This has been the case within the last few years, some writers of considerable ability having appealed to the history of Galileo in order to give point to opinions that they wished to advance. During all this time, if there has been unfairness on one side, there have been injudicious zeal and inaccuracy on the other.

These circumstances must form my apology for interfering in a dispute already so prolonged and so envenomed; and it has appeared to me that I may without presumption hope to amend the errors to which I have just alluded, if in no other way, at least by stating correctly the facts of the case. I do not, however, undertake to write a full biography of the great philosopher, or to give a detailed account of his numerous contributions to the scientific literature of his day; I confine myself principally to those great crises in his life, which have given rise to so much discussion, and which have chiefly contributed to make him a name in history.

GALILEO AND HIS JUDGES.

CHAPTER I.

BEFORE entering on any details relating to Galileo's life and works, I propose to give a brief sketch of the progress of astronomical knowledge up to his time; for without this, one cannot appreciate correctly the value of his contributions to science, a value exaggerated or underrated by different writers, each according to his respective bias.

The primitive conception of the Earth as a vast plain with the ocean flowing round it, and the solid firmament in the sky above it, with the Sun, Moon, and Stars driven across by some mysterious agency, need not be noticed from an astronomical point of view; it appeared naturally in ancient poetry and in the forms of speech adopted and continued by popular usage; but it is not necessary to dwell upon it.

The first astronomers with whom we are acquainted were the Greeks, though it is said by some writers that the Chaldeans and Egyptians were really the original astronomers of the ancient world, and what the Greeks knew was borrowed from them.

The vast majority of men from the earliest times down to the birth of Galileo believed that the Earth was the centre of the universe, round which the Sun, Moon, and Stars revolved every twenty-four hours; round which, also (as careful observers had perceived), the Sun had an annual motion, progressing through the various signs of the zodiac; moreover, it had been noticed that the planets moved round the Earth, though at widely differing periods.

Yet there had been some few men, exceptionally gifted, who had guessed (and truly so) that the popular conception was a wrong one. It is said that the old Greek philosopher, Pythagoras, taught his disciples that the Sun was the real centre of our system, and that the Earth and planets circulated round it; but he does not seem to have openly and explicitly published his doctrine, though the tradition of his having so taught has always existed. If he taught it, however, he stands almost alone among the ancients. There were two great authorities in particular, whose opinion carried immense weight, and who were both decided in holding that the Earth was the centre, and the Sun a revolving planet. The first of these, Aristotle, has exercised an influence over succeeding generations which is simply marvellous. How vast was the weight of his name as a philosopher in the age of the schoolmen is well known to every one who has ever glanced at the greatest work of the greatest intellect of that age, the "Summa" of

St. Thomas Aquinas. This celebrated writer quotes him as "philosophus," in his opinion *the philosopher par excellence*, and besides his general appreciation of him as thus shown, he wrote an elaborate treatise on the "Astronomy" of Aristotle.

Nor has this influence been confined to the schoolmen; it has remained ever since, even to this day and in this country, where in the University of Oxford his great work on ethics is still a standard book of study. At the time of Galileo, such was the reverence felt towards his authority in Italy and in Rome, that the Peripatetici, as those who specially belonged to his school were called, were probably quite as indignant with the revolutionary astronomer for disregarding the teaching of their philosopher, as for going counter to the literal interpretation of Scripture.

But in pure astronomy, apart from all other philosophy, the greatest of all ancient writers was Ptolemy, who in the second century of the Christian era wrote a work called the "Almagest," which is a complete compendium of the science as known at that date. Ptolemy probably borrowed very much from his great predecessor, Hipparchus, who has been called the father of astronomy, and who was the first to discover—to take a remarkable instance—the phenomenon known as the precession of the equinoxes, involving as it does the difference in length between the solar and sidereal years. The system of Ptolemy was briefly this: The heavens and the Earth are both spherical in form—the Earth being immovable in the centre, and all the heavenly motions taking place in circles. For this he gives his reasons—sound and good reasons for the spherical shape of the Earth; unsound and mistaken, however, for the denial of the Earth's rotation on its axis, an opinion he evidently knew had been maintained by some persons; one important argument on this latter head being that if the Earth rotated with the great velocity necessary to carry it round in one day, it would leave the air behind it. He places the Earth (as already said) in the centre, then the Moon as the nearest planet revolving round it, the next Mercury, then Venus, then the Sun, and beyond these Mars, Jupiter, and Saturn. All moved in circles, but since, with the exception of the Sun and Moon, simple circles would not account for the motions, he supposes small circles in a retrograde direction forming loops upon the main circle, which he calls *epicycles*; undoubtedly following in this respect, Hipparchus, who three centuries before had struck out the same idea. It is curious that Ptolemy's arguments (as above mentioned) show clearly that in his day there were some persons, though their names have perished,* some one or two philosophers endowed with a marvellous insight into Nature, who had guessed at the true solution of the great astronomical problem; but they left no enduring mark on their age. The system of Ptolemy accounted for

* Nicetas of Syracuse (whose date I am not able to give) seems to have been aware of the diurnal movement of the earth round its axis.

all the phenomena of the heavenly bodies that could be observed without the use of the telescope; naturally it held undisputed sway for many generations.

The first writer who revived the doctrine of Pythagoras as to the Earth's movement (if, indeed, Pythagoras ever really taught it) was Nicholas de Cusa; he was a German by birth, having, in fact, been born at Trèves, in 1401; but he was educated in Italy. He rose to a high ecclesiastical position, and was created cardinal by Pope Eugenius IV., in 1448; his book just alluded to was entitled "De Docta Ignorantia," and was dedicated to Cardinal Cesarini.

The first, however, whose work obtained any great notoriety, and who upheld the doctrine that the Earth revolved around the Sun, was Nicholas Kopernik, commonly called by the Latinised form of his name, Copernicus. He, too, was a German, born at Thorn, in 1473; he studied for a time at the University of Cracow, and like Nicholas de Cusa, afterwards in Italy, and was subsequently raised to the ecclesiastical dignity of a Canon. It is probable that he was not a priest (though he is frequently spoken of as such), but a Canon in minor orders. In 1500 he was appointed professor of mathematics at Rome; and such was his scientific reputation that he was consulted by the Council of Lateran, held in 1512, on the question of the reform of the calendar —a reform carried out at a later period by Pope Gregory XIII.

The system of Copernicus was well received at Rome. A German disciple of his, John Albert Widmanstadt, in the year 1533, expounded it before Pope Clement VII., and produced a very favourable impression. Nor was the favour shown to Copernicus and his teaching ever withdrawn at Rome; his great work, "De Revolutionibus Orbium Cœlestium" (published, it is said, by the advice of Cardinal Schunberg, Bishop of Capua), was dedicated to the reigning Pope, Paul III.; nor does he appear to have received at any time the least rebuke or discouragement from the Holy See; he died, however, immediately after the printing of his book, in May, 1543.

Copernicus supposed the heavenly bodies, the Earth included, to revolve round the Sun in *circles;* but, as it was evident that they did not exactly do this, he used the theory of epicycles, and supposed each planet to make two revolutions in each epicycle for every revolution round the Sun. The true solution of the difficulty was due to Kepler, who lived in the next century, and who discovered that the planets moved in *ellipses.* Copernicus held, and, of course, held truly, that the Earth revolves on its axis, thereby causing the apparent diurnal motion of all the heavenly bodies from east to west.

Owing to his work having been the first of any great importance that maintained argumentatively the system called *heliocentric*, that is to say, in which the Sun is the real centre, round which the planets, including the Earth, revolve—for the treatise of Nicholas de Cusa does not appear to have had any extensive circulation—it is usual to speak of this system as the *Copernican* one, notwithstanding the errors from which its great author was unable to extricate himself, and which have long since been rectified by subsequent writers; so that even at this day we retain the name.

It is always useful in scientific subjects to introduce a definition; and this is my definition of the sense in which I employ the word Copernican, that it is simply as opposed to the system in which the Earth is the centre of the visible universe, and the Sun revolving about it. It is, in fact, less accurate but more convenient than the employment of the Greek words heliocentric and geocentric to denote the two systems. Greek words, no doubt, abound in our scientific vocabulary, as the following plainly show: astronomy, geology, geography, barometer, thermometer, microscope, telescope; but these have become naturalised in our language by long use, which heliocentric and geocentric have not as yet been.

After Copernicus there arose an astronomer of great merit, a Dane, Tycho Brahé by name, who attempted to start a fresh system—a modification, in fact, of that of Ptolemy. He made all the planets revolve round the Sun, and the Sun, accompanied by the planets, round the Earth. He deserves great credit for his painstaking observations; but he lived just before the invention of the telescope—or, at least, before it was used for astronomical purposes—and, therefore, was under an infinite disadvantage. His chief objection to the system of Copernicus was one at which a modern astronomer would smile, but which in those days seemed very weighty—namely, the enormous distance at which you must suppose the fixed stars to be situated, if it were true. The philosophers of that age did not like to admit such a waste of space as that which must intervene between the orbit of Saturn and the stars. And, on the Copernican theory, if the stars were not situated at an immense, almost infinite distance, they ought to appear to move in a way they certainly do not. Tycho Brahé was born in 1546. His theory never made much way; it had not, I imagine, sufficient elements of probability to recommend it generally; while the subsequent invention of the telescope, and the works of Kepler and Galileo, coming so soon after Tycho Brahé, prepared the way for that almost universal reception of the Copernican system which we have since witnessed. I shall refer later on to Tycho and his observations.

Such, then, was the state of astronomical theories in the latter part of the sixteenth century. Enlightened men like Copernicus had guessed — not accurately, it is true, but with a considerable approach to accuracy—at the real facts of the case. Tycho Brahé (who, I suspect, would have been converted to Copernicanism if his life had been prolonged) had suggested a system of compromise not likely, in the long run, to satisfy any thoughtful mind; while the bulk of men, even the learned, adhered to the old Ptolemaic scheme. Something, however, now occurred which was destined to work, sooner or later, a complete revolution in astronomy. The telescope was invented, and, at the same time, there arose a man who knew how to use it: that man was Galileo. He was not the inventor of it, for it was first constructed in Holland or Belgium; yet he had the energy and the skill to make a telescope, without having previously seen one, simply from the account he had heard of the instrument. The telescope that he constructed, which still bears his name, was the simplest possible. It was of a form now disused excepting for opera-glasses and for the far more powerful binocular field-glasses with which we are so familiar; but for telescopes properly so called an improved principle has long since been introduced. Galileo was the first man that ever, so far as we know, turned the telescope upon the heavens. How he was rewarded for his pains we shall presently see; and I propose to introduce a narrative of the principal events in his life, since there are no means for forming a judgment so valuable as having the facts of the case clearly before the mind.

'For most of the facts I am indebted to M. Henri de l'Épinois, whose elaborate article in the French publication known as *La Revue des Questions Historiques* is of the highest value; as the author of this article has done what I suspect very few writers on Galileo have even attempted to do, namely, to inspect the documents preserved in the Vatican bearing on the process, some of which he gives at full length. Not having myself had the same advantage, I yet feel that I am treading on safe ground when I take my facts from M. de l'Épinois; for there is scarcely a statement that he makes for which he does not give his authority, whether from the documents just mentioned, or from Galileo's own letters, or from other trustworthy evidence.*

To treat of Galileo, and to pass over the events which brought him into collision with the ecclesiastical authorities, would of course be impossible, nor is it easy to touch upon these matters without having some standpoint of one's own — some principle to guide one, some basis from which to argue. I do not shrink from stating that I write from a Catholic standpoint; but without entering minutely into those subtle questions which are the province of the trained theologian.

As, however, a good deal of the narrative is connected with the action of the Roman Congregations, as they are termed, it may not be superfluous to explain briefly the nature of these institutions. They are formed by the selection of certain Cardinals, one of them acting as Prefect of the Congregation,

---

* M. de l'Épinois has, since then, published a still more complete collection of the various documents he had obtained permission to inspect at Rome; but this work is, unfortunately, out of print.

to whom are added other ecclesiastics as consultors and as secretary. The Congregation of the Index, to which reference will hereafter be made, was instituted not long after the Council of Trent, by Pope St. Pius V., and has for its duty, as its name implies, the pointing out to the faithful people such books as they ought to abstain from reading. The chief consultor of the Index is the "Master of the Apostolic Palace," whom I shall have occasion to mention more than once in connection with that Dialogue of Galileo which brought him into such serious disgrace at Rome.

The Congregation of the Inquisition—I need hardly say, not to be confounded with the Spanish tribunal of that name, which was founded at an earlier period, nor with similar tribunals in other countries—was erected in 1542 by Pope Paul III., and besides the other officials attached to it, had certain theologians called "qualifiers," whose duty it was to give an opinion to the Congregation on questions submitted to them.

These two Congregations, as well as several others which it is not necessary to enumerate, still exist, their functions being somewhat modified by the changing circumstances of the age. Their action is for the most part confined to matters of discipline, but they sometimes have questions of doctrine and moral obligation referred to them by the Pope, from whom, of course, they derive all authority that they possess.

I do not here undertake to show the advantage

and utility of these Congregations, or of any other institutions connected with the discipline of the Catholic Church. From the remarks I have just previously made, it will be understood that I take all this for granted, and that I feel justified in doing so. Those who differ from me will, I trust, excuse me when they find that this conviction on my part does not interfere with the impartial fairness of my narrative.

Galileo, whom I believe to have been a devout Catholic, would, if he were here to speak for himself, agree with me in principle, however he might complain of the action of the Roman Congregations in his own individual case.

We shall then, as we proceed, inquire whether this celebrated philosopher was, as some imagine, a hero and a martyr of science, or, as others think, a rash innovator, who happened by chance to be right, but who had little or nothing but vain and foolish arguments to adduce in support of his doctrines. Perhaps we shall find that such critics, on either side, are but imperfectly acquainted with the facts of the case.

CHAPTER II.

GALILEO GALILEI LINCEO—for such was his name in full—was born at Pisa, the 18th February, 1564. When about seventeen years old he commenced studying mathematics and physical science at the University of Pisa, and later on, in 1585, he came to Florence, in order to go through a mathematical course.

He seems to have been wholly free from the sceptical and irreligious spirit which unhappily warps the judgment of some scientific men in our own day. His moral conduct, however, in early life was not irreproachable, and it is recorded of him that he had a *liaison* with a lady named Maria Gamba, who became the mother of three children; but this illicit attachment did not last very long, and a separation took place, after which he saw Maria Gamba no more, and she was subsequently married to some other person. He then entered the celebrated monastery of Vallombrosa, where he was a novice for a short period; but, having apparently no vocation for the religious life, he left the monastery, and resumed his former pursuits. At the age of twenty-five he was appointed professor of mathematics at Pisa, the Grand Duke of Tuscany having invited him there on the recommendation of Cardinal del Monte. Here it was that he first excited hostility by attacking the theories of Aristotle on physical science, a thing not to be done with impunity in that age.

I have already alluded to the telescope constructed by Galileo, and it is scarcely necessary to say that such an instrument, however simple and rudimentary in its construction, could not fail to reveal to an intelligent observer truths hitherto unknown. It was discovered that the planet Jupiter had satellites, that Saturn had a ring, that Venus passed through phases like the moon, that there were spots on the Sun; this last discovery having been made about the same time by the learned Jesuit, Father Scheiner, and by Fabricius. It was not, I think, until the year 1610 that Galileo published his work called "Nuntius Siderius," in which he recounted the results he had obtained. This work seems to have provoked some considerable opposition, but Galileo was supported by the approbation of his patron, the Grand Duke of Tuscany. In the following year, 1611, he went to Rome, and here he was well received and treated with distinction by prelates of high position, and even by the Pope then reigning, Paul V. Moreover, when, in the year 1612, he published another work, which he called "Discorso sui Gallegianti," he met with general approval, and no less a person than Cardinal Maffei Barberini, who afterwards became Pope under the title of Urban VIII., is stated to have declared that he was in all points of the same opinion as Galileo.

Now it is quite true that incidental conversations, passing, perhaps, through the hands of two or three persons, are not to be greatly relied upon. It is also to be remarked that men in the position of Cardinals or ecclesiastics of high rank may often look with toleration and even favour on opinions stated in a guarded and hypothetical way, and yet, if called on to pronounce an official judgment on such opinions, would feel it a duty to pronounce against them. Nevertheless, there appears considerable reason for thinking that since Galileo's reputation stood so high, and his ability was so manifest, he would have escaped all censure if he had confined himself strictly to stating his views on the Copernican system as a scientific hypothesis, and had firmly resisted the temptation (strong as it was) to allow himself to be drawn into the Scriptural argument.

This, however, it must be remembered, was mainly the fault of his opponents. Unable to grapple with the question in its purely scientific aspect, some zealous anti-Copernicans turned to Holy Scripture for support—Scripture in its most rigid and literal interpretation; an interpretation, however, it must in fairness be stated, enshrined in the traditions of successive generations.

It is said that a monk named Sizi went so far as to maintain that the Bible contradicted the existence of the satellites of Jupiter. If this be true (which one cannot help doubting), we may well say that amongst all the perversions of Scripture in which human fancy has indulged, there is scarcely any one more monstrous; and we must not imagine that all the Biblical arguments used against Galileo and Copernicus were so unreasonable and exaggerated.

It was in 1613 that our philosopher published at Rome another work, entitled "L'Istoria e Dimostrazione Intorno alle Macchie Solari." It was, generally speaking, well received, though he drew a conclusion in favour of the Earth's rotation on its axis.

The controversy, however, became still keener on the all-important point of the interpretation of Scripture. Now that we can look back on the events of that day with all judicious calmness, we may well blame Galileo for having let himself fall into so dangerous a snare; but there was some excuse for him, attacked as he was on this very ground of the supposed incompatibility of his hypothesis with the teaching of Scripture; and so he unfortunately committed a grave error of judgment in grappling himself with a religious difficulty which, if wise, he would have left entirely to theologians. It may be said that this is not what we should naturally expect. We should suppose that the ecclesiastical authorities would welcome any attempt to prove that new scientific theories were not irreconcilable with the Scriptural narrative, and possibly such would be the case at the present day; but in those times it was certainly otherwise, and I am not quite sure whether the tone and tendency of Rome (that is to say, Rome as the centre of ecclesiastical tradition and authority) is not still, as it was then, in favour of the same rule of conduct—that, namely, which keeps a scientific man to his own province, and leaves to the authorities of the Church the duty of reconciling physical theories and speculations with the teaching of Holy Scripture. On this last-named point I need not say I speak with the utmost diffidence; but on the historical question, as to whether that was the feeling which animated Popes and Cardinals in Galileo's day, I think there can be very little doubt.

Now, as the controversy became embittered, a certain Father Cassini, a Dominican, preaching in the Church of Santa Maria Novella at Florence, attacked the Copernican doctrine as taught by Galileo; this aroused the wrath of the philosopher, and he wrote (on the 21st December, 1612) a letter to a Benedictine monk, Father Castelli, protesting against the interpretation of Scripture which Father Cassini had used; and while so protesting, overstepping, it appears, the limits of prudence. The result was that this unguarded letter was denounced by Father Lorini to the Cardinal Prefect of the Congregation of the Index.

The consequence of this was that in the early part of the year 1615 there commenced a process which in the following year had an important issue. It is said that in the month of March, 1615, Cardinal del Monte and Cardinal Bellarmine had a conversation on the subject of Galileo and his teaching, the result being that they both agreed on this one point: that Galileo ought to avoid entering on the interpretation of Scripture, this being a matter reserved to the ecclesiastical authorities.

Galileo was not then at Rome; and two influential friends of his, Mgr. Dini and Prince Cesi, advised him to be quiet and silent; such advice, however, was not to his taste, and he, on the contrary, thrust his head into the lion's mouth, confident of ultimate success. He came personally to Rome, mixed in society, and endeavoured by the use of such arguments as occurred to him in conversation to refute the ancient opinions. Several of his friends, including some of the Cardinals, advised moderation, but in vain; and such was his confidence in his cause, that in the early part of the year 1616 he actually began to complain of the delay in the process.

The Pope looked upon his conduct with evident displeasure, and it is stated in a letter of Guicciardini that on one occasion Cardinal Orsini spoke to him in favour of Galileo, and he answered that the Cardinal would do well to persuade his friend to abandon his opinion—adding that the affair was placed in the hands of the Cardinals of the Holy Office. After this incident, it is said, the Pope sent for Bellarmine, talked the matter over with him, and agreed that Galileo's opinion was erroneous and heretical. A decided step was now taken: on the 19th February, 1616, there was sent to certain theologians belonging to the Congregation of the Inquisition—technically called the *Qualifiers*—a copy of the propositions, the censure of which had been demanded: 1st, That the Sun was the centre of the world, and consequently immovable locally; 2nd, That the Earth was not the centre of the world, nor immovable, but moved round itself by a diurnal rotation.

The Qualifiers of the Congregation met on the 23rd February, and on the next day, in presence of the eleven theologians who had been consulted, the censure was pronounced. All declared that the first proposition was foolish and absurd, philosophically speaking, and also formally heretical, since it expressly contradicted numerous texts of Holy Scripture, according to the proper meaning of the words, and according to the ordinary interpretation and the sense admitted by the holy Fathers and theological doctors. All declared that the second proposition deserved the same censure philosophically, and regarding theological truth, that it was at least erroneous in point of faith. The next day, 25th February, Cardinal Mellinus notified to the Commissary of the Holy Office what had taken place, and the Pope desired Cardinal Bellarmine to send for Galileo, and admonish him to abandon the opinion in question; if he refused to obey, the Father Commissary, in presence of a notary and witnesses, was to enjoin upon him a command to abstain wholly from teaching such doctrine and opinion, from defending it, or treating of it; if,

c 2

however, he would not acquiesce, that he should then be imprisoned. On the following day, 26th February, this was accordingly done, and Galileo was warned "ut supra dictum opinionem . . . omnino relinquat, nec eam de cetero quovis modo doceat teneat aut defendat verbo aut scriptis," with the threat already mentioned in case of disobedience. Galileo promised to obey.

In the beginning of the month of March there appeared a printed decree of the Congregation of the Index prohibiting five works ; and here we arrive at the curious fact that no work whatever of Galileo was prohibited by name. The feeling in the high ecclesiastical circles of Rome seems at that time to have been very much to this effect : "Let us stamp out the obnoxious opinion, but let us spare Galileo individually." The final result (including what took place in after years) is strikingly contrasted with such expectations, if they existed. Galileo had to suffer personally, not bodily torture or incarceration, but humiliation and failure ; whilst the dreaded doctrine of Copernicanism, purified from incidental error and taught in an enlightened form, has triumphed and reigns supreme. The decree of the Index is particularly noteworthy, for it is the principal matter with which we have to deal. After prohibiting certain Protestant books, the decree proceeds as follows: "And since it has come to the knowledge of the above-named Sacred Congregation that that false Pythagorean doctrine, altogether con-

trary to Holy Scripture, concerning the movement
of the Earth and the immobility of the Sun, taught by
Nicolas Copernicus in his work on the Revolutions
of the Heavenly Orbs, and by Diego di Zunica in his
work on Job, is already spread about and received by
many persons, as may be seen in a printed letter
of a certain Carmelite Father, entitled 'A Letter
of the Rev. Father, Master Paul Anthony Foscarini,
on the opinion of the Pythagoreans and of Copernicus
respecting the mobility of the Earth and the stability
of the Sun, and the new Pythagorean System of
the World,' printed at Naples by Lazzaro Scorrigio,
1615, in which the said Father endeavours to show
that the aforesaid doctrine of the immobility of the Sun
in the centre of the universe and the mobility of the
Earth is consonant to the truth, and is not opposed
to Holy Scripture : Therefore, lest any opinion of
this kind insinuate itself to the detriment of Catholic
truth, [the Congregation] has decreed that the said
[works of] *Nicolas Copernicus on the Revolutions
of the Orbs* and *Diego di Zunica on Job* should
be suspended until they are corrected. But that
the book of Father Paul Anthony Foscarini the
Carmelite should be altogether prohibited and condemned; and that all other books teaching the same
thing should equally be prohibited, as by the present
decree it prohibits, condemns, and suspends them all
respectively. In witness whereof the present decree
has been signed and sealed by the hand and seal
of the Most Illustrious and Most Reverend Lord

Cardinal of Santa Cecilia, Bishop of Albano, on the 5th day of March, 1616."

Here follow the signatures:

"P. EPISC. ALBANEN.   CARD. SANCTÆ CÆCILIÆ.

"*Locus* ✠ *sigilli.*

"F. FRANCISCUS MAGDALENUS CAPIFERREUS,

"*Ord. Prædicat., Secretarius.*"

There followed a somewhat remarkable episode: some opponents of Galileo having spread a report that he had been compelled to make an abjuration, and also had had certain salutary penances inflicted on him, Cardinal Bellarmine gave him a certificate to the effect that nothing of the kind had taken place, but only that the declaration made by the Pope and published by the Congregation of the Index had been communicated to him; in which declaration was contained the statement that the doctrine attributed to Copernicus on the movement of the Earth round the Sun, and the stability of the Sun in the centre of the world without its moving from east to west, was contrary to Holy Scripture, and so could not be defended or held. It appears that the abjuration alluded to was a solemn act demanded only from those who were suspected of unsoundness in the faith, and carried with it some disgrace. Galileo was naturally anxious to be cleared from such imputation, and the authorities in Rome willingly met him so far, and avoided all acts casting a personal slur on him. It is noteworthy that the interview between Cardinal Bellarmine and Galileo took place after the answers had been returned by the Qualifiers of the Inquisition, but before the publication of the decree of the Index. The certificate given by the Cardinal, to which I have just alluded, was subsequent, and bears date the 26th May, 1616.

And here we may pause in the narrative, to inquire briefly what was the effect, in an ecclesiastical point of. view, of the decree just quoted, and of the admonition given by Papal order to Galileo. On the mere face of it, it cannot surely be maintained that there was any doctrinal decision, strictly speaking, at all. I do not wish to undervalue the importance of the disciplinary decision, I think it most momentous; moreover, the reason alleged for it was that the opinion, the publication of which was to be forbidden, was contrary to Scripture; but I fail to see how this last-mentioned fact can possibly convert what is avowedly a disciplinary enactment, prohibiting the circulation of certain books, into a dogmatic decree.

I should submit it to the judgment of theologians whether this would not be true even if the Pope's name had been explicitly introduced as sanctioning the decree; as it stands, however, the decree appears simply in the name of the Congregation of the Index.

It would, I think, scarcely be necessary to argue these points at length, were it not that the contrary view has been maintained in a work entitled "The

Pontifical Decrees against the Doctrine of the Earth's Movement, and the Ultramontane Defence of them," by the Rev. William W. Roberts, a work written with ability and moderation as well as considerable knowledge of the subject, since the author, though determined to make all the controversial capital that is possible out of the case of Galileo, rises superior to the vulgar atmosphere of fable and false accusation; never alleges anything like personal cruelty or ill-treatment as against the Pope or the Inquisition, and scarcely alludes to the mythical story of " E pur si muove."

Moreover, even were the intrinsic value of the work less than it is, attention has been publicly drawn to it by a writer whom, both from a religious and scientific point of view, we feel bound to treat with respect — Professor Mivart — although he has formed, on the other hand, an exaggerated estimate of the importance of Mr. Roberts' facts and arguments.

Here I wish to introduce an observation, as a sort of anticipatory self-defence, which is that I do not feel bound to enter into all the theological minutiæ which learned disputants have introduced into this case. Those who wish to sift such arguments in detail can read the articles in *The Dublin Review* by the late Dr. Ward (since republished) on the one hand, and Mr. Roberts' book on the other. I myself venture to look at the question as a lay theologian, employing this expression not by any means in the sense of one who, having read two or three theological treatises, presumes to discuss the sacred science, himself an amateur, with men whose profession it is to teach theology; for, to use a familiar expression, I hope I know my place better. I employ the word in the sense of a man who seeks to know what the Church teaches as requisite for a layman, that is an *educated* layman, to understand: thus the lay theologian, as I consider him, ought to be able to discriminate between what the Church teaches him as matter of faith and what she enjoins or encourages him to hold under a less solemn sanction. He ought also to distinguish clearly between matters laid down by the Church as parts of her definitive teaching both on faith and morals—points, that is to say, laid down as of *principle*, and therefore irrevocable—and on the other hand matters of discipline which, whether intrinsically important or not, may and do vary from age to age. He may of course make mistakes, as even theologians may do, in applying his principles to particular cases; but he ought to understand what the principles are.

Now applying such plain principles to the Galileo case, I do not understand how any one can come to any other conclusions than these: first, that the decree of the Index and the other proceedings in 1616, though founded on reasons of doctrine, that is of the correct interpretation of Scripture, were purely disciplinary in their nature; secondly, that this being so, they were not infallible or *irreform-*

able, as the term is; thirdly, that they were, however, real acts of discipline, and intended to be enforced more or less stringently according to circumstances. This last-named aspect of the case is a matter of importance, and I shall return to it hereafter; but the attempt to impugn the doctrinal infallibility of the Catholic Church on the strength of such decisions as that of the Index in 1616, seems to me so groundless that I should not discuss the question further were it not that I think it right to notice some of Mr. Roberts' arguments.

It appears that certain theologians have held that decrees of the Roman Congregations are to be considered infallible, provided they contain a statement in so many words that the Pope has approved them, and provided also that they have been published by his explicit order. This, it may be mentioned, does not necessarily imply that such decrees concern matters which are strictly and technically matters of *faith*, other less momentous issues being frequently involved.

The decree of the Index in 1616 had no such statement about the Pope's approbation, nor any notice of his express order for its publication, although, in reality, it was undoubtedly approved by him. Mr. Roberts argues that this distinction is a worthless one, because, at that time, the custom, since adopted on certain important occasions, of bringing in the Pope's name and authority explicitly, had not come into being.

As an *argumentum ad hominem* against certain writers who have suggested that such an omission in the Galileo case was a remarkable instance of Divine Providence, Mr. Roberts' answer may stand; but it has nothing to do with the main argument. It only shows that whereas the Popes of more modern times have employed the Roman Congregations as instruments for conveying to the world their own decrees on certain doctrinal subjects, the Popes of the early part of the seventeenth century had no such custom. They used the Congregations for various disciplinary purposes, founded sometimes, no doubt, on reasons of doctrine, and they sanctioned the proceedings so taken; but they did not give them the explicit impress of their own name and authority. Even when this latter has taken place, it is not every theologian who holds that such decree is infallible. Cardinal Franzelin, a writer of the highest authority, whose words I give in a note,* held that it was not in-

---

* "Principium 7ᵐ.—Sancta Sedes Apostolica cui divinitus commissa est custodia depositi, potestas pascendi universam Ecclesiam ad salutem animarum, potest sententias theologicas vel quatenus cum theologicis nectuntur proscribere ut sequendas vel proscribere ut non sequendas, non unice ex intentione definitivâ sententiâ infallibiliter decidendi veritatem, sed etiam absque illa ex necessitate et intentione vel simpliciter vel pro determinatis adjunctis prospiciendi *securitati*[1] doctrinæ Catholicæ. In hujusmodi declarationibus licet non sit doctrinæ *veritas infallibilis*, quia hanc decidendi ex hypothesi non est intentio; est tamen *infallibilis*

[1] "Non coincidere hæc duo, infallibilem veritatem et securitatem, manifestum est vel ab eo, quod secus nulla doctrina probabilis aut probabilior posset dici sana et secura."

fallibly true, but only infallibly safe. His language is not quite clear to the non-theological mind, but he probably meant that the doctrine conveyed in such a decree was safe, so that it might certainly be held without injury to any one's faith, and that it was not safe to reject it. But it is clear that he was not speaking of such decrees as took place in the Galileo case, but only of those which bear on them the marks of Papal authority in the strict sense.

His own words are pretty plain proof of this. They are extracted from his work, "De Divina Traditione et Scriptura," and follow the other words to which I have alluded:

Coroll. D. Auctoritas infallibilitatis et supremum magisterium Pontificis definientis omnino nihil unquam pertinuit ad causam Galilei Galilei, et ad ejurationem opinionis ipsi injunctam. Non solum enim nulla vel umbra definitionis Pontificiæ ibi intercessit, sed in toto illo decreto Cardinalium S. Officii, et in formula ejurationis ne nomen quidem Pontificis unquam sive directe sive

securitas. Securitatem dico tum objectivam doctrinæ declaratæ [vel simpliciter vel pro talibus adjunctis], tum subjectivam quatenus omnibus tutum est eam amplecti, et tutum non est, nec absque violatione debitæ submissionis erga magisterium divinitus constitutum fieri potest, ut eam amplecti recusent.

"Coroll. C. Falsum est, auctoritatem propter quam debeatur assensus intellectus, solam esse auctoritatem Dei revelantis seu Ecclesiæ vel Pontificis infallibiliter definientis; sunt enim gradus assensus religiosi multiplices. In præsenti distinguendus est assensus *fidei proprie et immediate divinæ* propter auctoritatem Dei revelantis; assensus fidei quam supra diximus *mediate divinam* propter auctoritatem infallibilitur definientis doctrinam ut veram non tamen ut revelatam; assensus *religiosus* propter auctoritatem universalis providentiæ ecclesiasticæ in sensu declarato."—*De Divina Traditions et Scriptura*, p. 116, et seq. Ed. 1870.

indirecte pronuntiatum reperitur. .... pertinebat omnino ad *auctoritatem providentiæ ecclesiasticæ* cavere, ne quid detrimenti caperet interpretatio Scripturæ per conjecturas et hypotheses plerisque tum temporis visas minime verisimiles.

We are not, however, I think, obliged to endorse the opinion conveyed in the last sentence that I have quoted, though certain theologians of great weight have held that the ecclesiastical authorities of Galileo's day were only acting with proper prudence in the then existing state of astronomical knowledge. I shall hereafter state why I feel it difficult to follow their judgment.

But the words I have quoted from Cardinal Franzelin show plainly that the decrees he had in his mind, when he wrote that they were infallibly safe, were of a nature quite different from anything that took place in the processes connected with Galileo; and although he alludes principally to that which passed in 1633 before the Inquisition, he appears to include the whole affair in the judgment he passes upon it; indeed, the sentence of the tribunal in 1633, and the abjuration enjoined upon Galileo at that time, were made to depend on the decree of the Index in 1616, and the admonition then given to Galileo by Cardinal Bellarmine. Cardinal Franzelin's opinion, then, whatever weight we may give to it, is clear enough.

I give one more extract from the work of this learned author on the subject of the Pope's infallibility, showing that he was of opinion that doctrinal definitions must be clearly and unmistakably intended as such, and must carry with them some manifest signs to that effect.

Extract from the same on the subject of the Pope's infallibility, pp. 108 and 109:

> Neque enim *Cathedra Apostolica* aliud est, quam supremum authenticum magisterium, cujus definitiva sententia doctrinalis obligat universam Ecclesiam ad consensum. Intentio hæc definiendi doctrinam seu docendi definitivâ sententiâ et auctoritate obligante universam Ecclesiam ad consensum debet esse manifesta et cognoscibilis claris indiciis.

In the case we have before us, I should say that the "clara indicia" were all the other way; and indeed, were it not for the dust which controversialists have tried to throw in our eyes, I should be disposed to add that we might fairly drop this part of our subject—I mean the part which raises the question whether there was not some decision or definition, such as Catholics are bound by their principles to admit as infallible, given against the Copernican doctrine.

It is right, however, to notice one or two other arguments urged by Mr. Roberts.

Some of these consist in bringing forward supposed parallel cases, in which the Pope has insisted on a full and complete assent being given to the decision of some Roman Congregation. One case is that of a "distinguished theologian and philosopher, Günther," whose works were condemned by a decree of the Index, having, however, the notice that the Pope had ratified the decision and ordered its publication. This was in 1857. Günther and many of his followers submitted, but others contended that a merely disciplinary decree was not conclusive. On this Pope Pius IX. addressed a brief to the Archbishop of Cologne, in which he intimated that a decree sanctioned by his authority and published by his order should have been sufficient to close the question, that the doctrine taught by Günther could not be held to be true, and that it was not permitted to any one to defend it from that time forward.

I extract the words as given by Mr. Roberts:

> Quod quidem Decretum [that of the Index] Nostra Auctoritate sancitum Nostroque jussu vulgatum, sufficere plane debebat, ut questio omnis penitus dirempta censeretur, et omnes qui Catholico gloriantur nomine clare aperteque intelligerent sibi esse omnino obtemperandum, et sinceram haberi non posse doctrinam Güntharianis libris contentam, ac nemini deinceps fas esse doctrinam iis libris traditam tueri ac propugnare, et illos libros sine debita facultate legere ac retinere.

Mr. Roberts, it must be remembered, is not simply investigating the history of Galileo, but is contending, for other reasons, against certain opinions on the subject of Papal infallibility held by an able foreign theologian, M. Bouix, and by Dr. Ward, and he uses Galileo as a weapon (and, in his estimation, a most formidable weapon) in the controversy. Now, in the capacity I have assumed of a *lay theologian*, I do not feel bound to discuss whether the decree in Günther's case was merely disciplinary, or whether it was dogmatic; whether it came within the category of strictly infallible pronouncements, or whether it did not; and supposing the former alternative, whether it was infallible in virtue of the Pope's sanction and command to publish in the first instance, or whether it only became so in virtue of the brief addressed to the Archbishop of Cologne. All these questions, interesting in themselves, I feel myself at liberty to pass over, and to leave them, with the most profound respect, to be sifted by professed theologians; I merely venture to remark, without attempting to argue the matter, that, to my uninstructed intelligence, the whole thing, including the Pope's brief, appears to have a disciplinary character rather than anything else.

What, however, I would say is this—the questions above mentioned, which in the Günther case are doubtful, are in that of Galileo clear enough; the clause stating that the Pope had sanctioned the decree, and ordered it to be published, on which the doubt alluded to is founded, did not appear in the decree against the Copernican books; nor did the Popes of that day issue any brief, such as Pius IX. addressed to the Archbishop of Cologne.

Mr. Roberts, it is true, thinks he has a clenching argument in a Bull of Pope Alexander VII., of which I will speak hereafter, and which in my humble judgment has the least force of any that he has adduced.

The case of Professor Ubaghs, of the University of Louvain, which Mr. Roberts thinks still more to the point, seems, I confess, to me even weaker than the other for our present purpose. Here, again, I leave it to theologians to decide whether the decree was or was not infallible ; but it undoubtedly appears, in point of form, to be a doctrinal one, and emanated from the United Congregations of the Index and Inquisition, to whom the Pope had expressly entrusted the examination of the subject, and it was as follows : " Wherefore the most eminent cardinals have arrived at this opinion : that in the philosophical works, hitherto published by G. C. Ubaghs, and especially in his Logic and Theodicea, doctrines or opinions are found that cannot be taught without danger" (*inveniri doctrinas seu opiniones, quæ absque periculo tradi non possunt*). Which judgment our most Holy Lord Pope Pius IX. has ratified and confirmed by his supreme authority." Even then some persons maintained that the decree was disciplinary and not doctrinal. Cardinal Patrizi, however, writing in the Pope's name to the Primate of Belgium (if I mistake not), intimated that the dissentients must acquiesce *ex animo* in the judgment of the Apostolic See. Consequently all the professors who had committed themselves to the proscribed opinions were required to make an act of submission to the effect just mentioned. The decree was treated as strictly doctrinal, and if so was, I maintain, essentially different from the one we have now before us.

In the case of Galileo, it is true that the opinion given in 1616 by the Qualifiers of the Inquisition was a doctrinal one; the action taken upon the strength of that opinion by the Pope in desiring Cardinal Bellarmine to admonish Galileo, as well as by the Congregation of the Index in prohibiting certain books, was simply disciplinary.*

It remains for us to inquire what was the value of the decree of the Index on certain works, written in favour of the new astronomical doctrines, as appreciated by *contemporary* feeling and opinion. We naturally find that there were two views on the subject: one of those who wished to magnify the effect of the decision, and one of those who desired to minimise it.

Galileo himself said that his opinion had not been accepted by the Church, which, however, had only declared that it was not in conformity with Holy Scripture; from which it followed that only books attempting *ex professo* to prove that the opinion is not contrary to Scripture were prohibited. Whether Galileo was right or wrong in his estimate of the scope of the decree, it seems evident that he considered the whole matter as a question merely of discipline.

It is said that Father Melchior Inchofer, S.J. (afterwards one of the Consultors of the Holy Office),

---

* It happens, curiously enough, that the doctrine of the perfect immobility of the Sun, which so shocked the Qualifiers of the Inquisition, is simply discarded by modern astronomers. No one now holds that the Sun is the centre of the whole universe, or that he is immovable. It is generally supposed that he travels in space, though not round any *known* centre, and the Earth and Planets with him.

endeavoured to prove that the decision proceeded from the Pope speaking *ex cathedrâ*. Mr. Roberts gives a quotation to that effect from a work of Professor Berti; the original, however, does not appear, and is probably not now extant.

Mr. Roberts also quotes Caramuel, "the acute casuist," who, in answer to the supposed objection that the Copernican theory might hereafter be shown to be true, says that it is impossible that the Earth should hereafter be proved demonstratively to be in motion; if such an impossibility be admitted, other impossible and absurd things would follow.

Caramuel, however great as a theologian, was evidently not endowed with much scientific foresight. But he is not wholly wrong, for it has never yet been possible to prove by *absolute demonstration* the motion of the Earth.

One of the most important witnesses on the point we are here considering is Cardinal Bellarmine, who was a very zealous anti-Copernican, and had probably a great share (perhaps the principal share) in bringing about the practical condemnation of Galileo's opinions in 1616. So far as I know, the only explicit statement bearing on the question that we have of Bellarmine's, is a letter to the Carmelite Father Foscarini, dated April 1, 1615, though he has been quoted as if he had expressed the opinion stated in the letter at a later date. Mr. Roberts takes exception to the inference drawn from this letter because it was written before the decree of the Index, and we may add, about seven months before the referring of Galileo's writings to the Consultors of the Inquisition.

Now we may admit that there would be some force in this argument if Cardinal Bellarmine, instead of being what he was, had been a private individual, having nothing to do but to listen submissively to what his ecclesiastical superiors decided, whether in doctrine or discipline. He was, however, one of the most trusted advisers of the Pope; he had no small share in bringing about the censure of the Copernican theory, such as it was; and it is almost certain that at the time when he wrote the letter he foresaw that some proceedings of that nature would follow, if indeed the proceedings had not already begun. We have no sort of intimation that he ever afterwards changed his opinion, and the way in which he was quoted by subsequent writers points to this conclusion. I have thought it better to answer the objection made by Mr. Roberts before stating what Bellarmine's letter contains. I must leave my readers to judge the value of the argument. All I say is, that my own belief is that Cardinal Bellarmine's opinion, as recorded in this letter to Father Foscarini, represents his permanent judgment. It is a most curious letter, and is a singular illustration of the danger that a man, however able and learned, may incur by attempting to grapple with subjects of which he knows absolutely nothing. Bellarmine, when writing on theological or controversial subjects, though he might make an occasional mistake, was one of the clearest, ablest, and (may one not add?) fairest of writers; but on a subject such as this, some of his reasoning strikes us as very curious.

The substance of it is as follows: After admitting that so long as the Copernican doctrine is stated hypothetically, "*ex suppositione*," there is no objection whatever to it, he goes on to say that to state it positively and as a reality is contrary to the principle laid down by the Council (*i.e.* of Trent), that Scripture should not be interpreted contrary to the common consent of the Fathers; and, he added, not only that, but the universal opinions of modern commentators. In answer to the objection that it is not a matter of faith, he says: "if it is not so *ex parte objecti*, it is so *ex parte dicentis*," meaning apparently that a man who impugned the truth of the Scriptural narrative in any respect would be heretical. Then follows the paragraph which has given occasion to quote the letter, and it is to this effect:* When there shall be a real demonstration that the Sun stands in the centre of the universe, and that the Earth revolves round it, it will then be necessary to proceed with great consideration in explaining those passages of Scripture

---

* "Dico, che quando ci fosse vera dimostratione che il Sole stia nel centro del mondo, e la terra nel 3 cielo, e che il Sole non circonda la terra, ma la terra circonda il Sole, allora bisogneria andar con molta consideratione in esplicare le Scritture che paiono contrarie, e più tosto dire che non l' intendiamo, che dira che sia falso quello che si dimostra. Ma io non crederò che ci sia tale dimostratione fin che non mi sia mostrata, etc."—*Extract from Cardinal Bellarmine's Letter to F. Foscarini.*

which seem to be contrary to it, and rather to say that we do not understand them, than say that a thing which is demonstrated is false. But for his own part, until it had been shown to him, he would not believe there could be any such demonstration, for it was one thing to prove that if the hypothesis were true all things would appear as they actually do, and another thing to prove that such is actually the fact; and in case of doubt one ought not to leave the interpretation of Scripture as given by the Fathers. Then comes what is really an extraordinary argument, as we modern thinkers would view it. The text, "The sun arises and sets, and returns to his own place," was written by Solomon, who was not only inspired by God, but was also the wisest and most learned of mankind in human sciences, and in the knowledge of created things, and it was not likely he could be wrong. Nor was it sufficient to say that Solomon speaks according to appearances; for though in some cases erroneous impressions, arising from appearances, can be corrected by observation and experience, it is quite otherwise as regards the motion of the Earth.

It is certainly remarkable that it does not appear to strike Bellarmine that the Fathers and commentators, not having this question before them, naturally interpreted Scripture according to the ideas generally entertained in their day. While to suppose that, because Solomon wrote certain inspired works, and, moreover, was a great naturalist--the greatest of his day — he was, therefore, infallible in his personal views on astronomy, shows a state of mind so different from what we find amongst even non-scientific men in our own day, that we are almost startled and bewildered when we meet with it. The truth, however, is that Bellarmine was a sort of link between the mediæval and modern thinkers; in theology and controversy, and in appreciation of the change that had taken place in Europe owing to the religious revolution of the preceding century, in all that, he was, I imagine, in advance of his age; in physical science he was a simple mediævalist. But it was not for some time that even able men came to recognise the principle that in the search for truth, so far as the works of Nature are concerned, the opinions of the ancients and the traditions of forefathers count but for little; and observation and experiment are the true and only key to knowledge. It is otherwise, of course, with theology and kindred studies; and it required some mental grasp, or in default of that it required a long, very long, experience before the human mind drew the distinction between the two.

But this is a digression. I have quoted Bellarmine to show what he thought of the necessity, from an ecclesiastical standpoint, of putting down Copernicanism, at least until it should be proved to demonstration. He did not appear to contemplate a dogmatic decision against it, but what he did desire, and succeeded in obtaining, was a disciplinary prohibition of the obnoxious doctrine. As a theologian he well knew that such a prohibition would not be an irrevocable act ; it might be withdrawn when the conclusive proof of the forbidden opinion should be established. He probably thought that the certain demonstration of the opinion would only take place, as mathematicians would say, at an infinitely distant date ; nor was he wholly wrong, as has already been remarked, for the absolute demonstration of the Copernican doctrine is not, from the very nature of the case, a thing to be achieved.

Yet, if he had lived at a later period, I do not doubt that he would have been satisfied with the moral evidence, the mass of indirect proof, on which Copernicanism rests. Many years later, the Jesuit Father Fabri, who appears to have held the office of Canon Penitentiary of St. Peter's, expresses himself in much the same way as Bellarmine. He was replying to the arguments of some Copernican correspondent, possibly an Englishman, since his reply was inserted in the Acts of the English Royal Society in 1665, and he says: "There is no reason why the Church should not understand those texts in their literal sense, and declare that they should be so understood so long as there is no demonstration to prove the contrary. But if any such demonstration hereafter be devised by your party (which I do not at all expect), in that case the Church will not at all hesitate to set forth that those texts are to be understood in an improper—*i.e.*, non-literal—and figurative sense, according to the words of the poet, 'terræque urbesque recedunt.'"

As a further illustration of the position thus taken by Bellarmine and others as to the interpretation of Scripture, I may here mention that some few years after the prohibition of Copernican works by the Index (probably about 1623), it is said that Guidacci had an interview with Father Grassi, at the suggestion of the Jesuit Father Tarquinio Galluzzi, and that F. Grassi's words were as follows: "When a demonstration of this movement [that of the Earth] shall be discovered, it will be fitting to interpret Scripture otherwise than has hitherto been done: this is the opinion of Cardinal Bellarmine." It is not intended to deny that there were those who magnified the effect of the decree of the Index; the devotees of Aristotle, who had gained what was to them a great triumph, were sure to make the most of it.

CHAPTER III.

WE will now return to the narrative; and in due course discuss the condemnation of Galileo by the Inquisition sixteen years after the events just described.

It may be mentioned, as illustrating the feeling in Rome towards Galileo personally, that on the 11th March, 1616, he had an audience, lasting three-quarters of an hour, of Pope Paul V. He assured the Pope of the rectitude of his intentions, and complained of the persecutions of his adversaries. Paul V. answered very kindly, saying that both himself and the Cardinals of the Index had formed a high personal opinion of him, and did not believe his calumniators.

In the year 1620 there appeared a monitum of the Congregation of the Index, permitting the reading of the great work of Copernicus after certain specified corrections had been made.

Not long after this, in 1622, if I mistake not, Pope Paul V. died, and Galileo's friend, Cardinal Barberini, succeeded him, taking the name of Urban VIII.

Another of his friends, Monsignor Ciampoli, became secretary of briefs to the new Pope.

Our philosopher having ascertained that he would be well received, went to Rome in April, 1624, and was treated by the new Pope with all possible consideration. He had, in fact, several conversations with him; and we may well conjecture it was on these occasions that Urban VIII., discussing the Copernican theory, used some of those arguments which Galileo afterwards put in the mouth of Simplicio in his celebrated Dialogue, thereby deeply offending the Pope.

But there was, about this time, a sort of moderate reaction in favour of Galileo among the authorities at Rome. For instance, a work of his published since the decree of the Index, and entitled "Il Saggiatore," in which he had favoured the theory of the Earth's motion, was attacked, and an attempt was made to have it prohibited or at least corrected, but the attempt was a failure.

The reports of casual or unofficial conversations are always to be received with caution and with some qualification; yet at least they are "straws which show how the wind blows."

Thus we are told that Cardinal Hohen-Zollern, in a conversation with the Pope (Urban VIII.) on the subject of Copernicus, endeavoured to show the necessity of proceeding with great circumspection on that point, to which it is said the Pope replied that the Church had not condemned and would not condemn that opinion as heretical, but only as temerarious. So again the Master of the Sacred Palace, himself resting neutral between Ptolemy and Copernicus, is reported to have said that there was no matter of faith in question, the great point being that one must not in any way mix up the Holy Scriptures with it.

We may suppose that when the Pope spoke of the opinion having been condemned as temerarious, what he meant was not that it had been explicitly censured as such—using the word in the technical sense which it bears when applied as a censure—for that it plainly had not been, but that the general effect of the prohibition issued by the Index was to stamp the mark of rashness upon it. This, I may observe, if it be the right interpretation, is quite consistent with the theory that the prohibition was of a disciplinary and a provisional character.

We have also another reputed conversation of the Pope with Campanella—resting on the authority of Prince Cesi, who related it to Father Castelli—and it is important if true. Campanella had said that certain Germans, ready to embrace the Catholic faith, had hesitated on account of the condemnation of Copernicus, to which Pope Urban VIII. had replied that this was not his intention, and if he had had the arrangement of matters the decree would never have been made. "Non fu mai nostra intenzione; e se fosse toccato a noi, non si sarebbe fatto quel decreto."

As already remarked, we must not attach too great weight to reports of private conversations; but it is probable that some such scene took place as here represented, and, if it did, it is surely wholly incompatible with the idea that the decree was a decision in matters of faith. No Pope, no well-informed ecclesiastic of any rank, would express himself so in such a case; but it is quite consistent with what we might expect in a question of simple discipline.

It will now be convenient, before discussing the matter further, to resume the narrative, and to touch upon the questions connected with the condemnation of Galileo by the Inquisition, and his enforced abjuration. It is, indeed, these latter proceedings that have left so deep an impression upon the popular mind, though, strictly speaking, they were of less importance than the decree of the Index—of less importance, that is, to all others besides Galileo himself.

It seems that our philosopher overrated the effect of the reaction that had taken place in his favour, real though it was so far as it went. He thought he might now safely publish the work on which he had been labouring, and on which he probably relied as likely to influence the minds of learned men, ecclesiastical as well as lay, in the direction of Copernicanism.

He came in May in the year 1630 to Rome, and had a very long audience with the Pope, who treated him with great kindness and even increased a pension he had already bestowed upon him; but we do not know what passed as to other matters on this occasion. He had also an interview with Father Riccardi, who had now become Master of the Sacred Palace, with a view of obtaining authority to print his book. Father Riccardi upon this engaged Father Visconti, who was a professor of mathematics, to read the work and mark such passages as he thought necessary.

Father Visconti reported that there were some passages which required correction, and many points that he would like to discuss with the author. However, the Master of the Sacred Palace gave leave for the printing of the work, expressing at the same time a wish to see it once more himself; consequently it was arranged that Galileo should return to Rome in the autumn, in order to add the preface, and to insert in the body of the work certain passages, calculated to show that the question was being treated purely as a hypothesis.

Two untoward events, however, now occurred: one was the death of Prince Cesi, a powerful and devoted friend of Galileo, which took place on the 1st May; and the other was the outbreak of the plague at Florence, a circumstance which interrupted communications, and caused delays resulting in mistakes and misunderstandings. With a view of having the Dialogue printed at Florence, it was arranged that the revision required by the ecclesiastical authorities should take place there instead of at Rome. Father Hyacinthe Stephani, a Dominican, who acted as reviser, marked several passages in the work, thinking that they should be explained before the final permission for publication was conceded.

Then followed mutual delays: the author was tardy

in sending to Rome the corrections to which he had in principle agreed, and the Master of the Sacred Palace was late in sending to Florence the preface and the conclusion, so the impatient philosopher began to print his book. The plague still continued, and the result was that communications were still interrupted.

The Inquisitor of Florence however received from Rome the power to approve officially the copy of Galileo's work that would be submitted to him, with instructions specially added by Father Riccardi that he must bear in mind the wishes of the Pope to the following effect: The title of the work must indicate that it dealt only with the mathematical question connected with Copernicanism, also that the Copernican opinion must not be put forward as a positive truth, but merely as a hypothesis, and this without alluding to the interpretation of Scripture; moreover, that it should be stated that the work was only written to show that if the decree (*i.e.* of 1616) was made at Rome, nevertheless the authorities knew all the reasons against it that could be urged, and were not ignorant of one of them—an idea conformable to the words of the preface and the conclusion, which he would send from Rome corrected. With this precaution, it was intimated the book would meet with no obstacle at Rome, and thus satisfaction might be given to the author, and also to the Grand Duke of Tuscany, who had shown himself to be so eager in the matter.

This remarkable letter points towards a conclusion

which has been drawn by some writers, that the preface to the Dialogue was written for Galileo by Father Riccardi or some other person, and was not his own composition; for the above is precisely what was said in the preface as it afterwards appeared, and it seems to me almost incredible that Galileo should have spontaneously written any such words, exposing him to the charge, which has really been made against him, of transparent irony, thereby giving offence in the very quarters where conciliation was desirable.

And it must be remarked that when Father Riccardi on the 19th July of this year sent the preface to Florence, he allowed Galileo the liberty of making verbal alterations only; so that whether he composed it or only revised it, it is Father Riccardi rather than the author of the Dialogue who must be held responsible for the contents, and the same remark applies at least partially to the conclusion also, it having been specially revised by the same hand.

The preface is addressed to the discreet reader, and the words to which I have just alluded are as follows: "Some years ago, a wholesome edict was promulgated in Rome which, in order to check the dangerous scandals of the present age, imposed an opportune silence upon the Pythagorean opinion of the motion of the earth. There were not wanting some who rashly asserted that that decree resulted, not from judicious examination, but from ill-informed passion; and there were heard complaints that Consulters, wholly inexperienced in astronomical observations, ought not to be allowed, with a hasty prohibition, to clip the wings of speculative intellects. My zeal could not keep silence on hearing the temerity of the complaints so made. As one fully informed of that most prudent decision, I judged it right to appear publicly in the theatre of the world, as a witness of pure truth. I happened then to be present in Rome; I had not only audiences, but approbations from the most eminent prelates of that Court, and it was not without my own previous information that the publication of that decree then followed." The author goes on to say that he wished to show to foreign nations how much was known in Italy, and particularly in Rome, on this subject; and that from this climate there proceed not only dogmas for the salvation of the soul, but ingenious devices for the delight of the mind.

This last clause certainly savours of bitter irony, and probably did not proceed from Father Riccardi's pen. He then states that for the purpose in hand he had taken the Copernican part in the Dialogue as a pure mathematical hypothesis, endeavouring by every artifice to represent it as superior, not to that of the stability of the Earth absolutely speaking, but to the doctrine as defended by the Peripatetics, to whom he alludes with some contempt.

He adds that he will treat of three principal heads: under the first he would show that all our experience was insufficient to prove conclusively the motion of the Earth, but that it adapted itself equally to either theory; he hoped also to produce many observations unknown to antiquity. In the second place, the celestial phenomena would be examined, by which the Copernican hypothesis would be so reinforced as if it ought to come out of the contest absolutely victorious. In the third place he would propound his theory about the tides; "proporrò una fantasia ingegnosa," he says. He had long been of opinion that the unknown problem of the tides would receive some light on the assumption of the Earth's motion. Other persons had adopted his statement on this point as if it had been their own; he therefore thought it desirable to expound it himself. He hints, too, that the willingness to admit the stability of the Earth, and to take the contrary side solely for mathematical caprice, is partly based on piety, religion, the knowledge of the Divine omnipotence, and the consciousness of human weakness.

He had thought it well to cast these thoughts into the form of a dialogue, which gave a certain amount of freedom to digressions.

He then introduces the personages who sustain the discussion, and who are supposed to meet at Venice at the palace of one of their number, Sagredo by name.

This preface, if one may judge by internal evidence, was probably the joint composition of Galileo and Father Riccardi, the former having written the original draft, the latter having altered the draft and supplemented it with important additions.

The body of the Dialogue—which I suspect that many persons who consider themselves competent to give an opinion on the Galileo case have not so much as even seen—is divided into four portions, each being supposed to be one day's dialogue. The interlocutors are Salviati, Sagredo, and Simplicio. Great offence was taken at the rôle attributed to this last-named personage—the true doctrine put into the mouth of a simpleton! It has been said that Pope Urban VIII. considered it as an insult directed against himself, because, in conversation with Galileo, he had used some of the very arguments employed by Simplicio. This, however, may have happened without the author intending thereby to offer any personal affront to His Holiness; some character was bound to appear on the anti-Copernican side, and it was inevitable that the arguments that Galileo had heard, whether from ignorant or enlightened antagonists, should be put into the mouth of such character. The name Simplicio is of course not meant as a compliment; moreover, he is made to say some very unwise things, and is occasionally treated with a sort of polite contempt by the scientific and mathematical Salviati; and yet he is not at all a simpleton in our sense of the word, he is a devoted follower of Aristotle, whom he constantly quotes, and is in fact a type — probably exaggerated—of the school of the Peripatetics, as they were, and still are, called; he does not know much of geometry or arithmetic, and so is at no small disadvantage when arguing with Salviati, but he is far from being a mere fool. Our author, in his preface, introduces Salviati and Sagredo—the former a Florentine, the latter a Venetian—as real personages, deceased friends of his own, though this may be a mere conventional form of expression; but he expressly states that Simplicio is not the true name of the "buon Peripatetico."

The friends are supposed to meet in the palace of Sagredo, at Venice, as before stated.

The first day's dialogue deals with a good deal of what one may term preliminary matter: that bodies have three dimensions and no more; that circular motion is the most perfect and the most natural; showing by this that Galileo had not at that time arrived at a true comprehension of the first law of motion, as we now hold it. The motion of weights on an inclined plane finds also a place in the discussion; and so does what we now term the law of accelerating force, which Galileo had grasped so well as to be able to explain how the velocity increases by infinitely small steps gradually, and not, as it were, by sudden jumps.

Much of the matter disputed on—as, for example, whether the heavenly bodies being incorruptible differ in that respect from the Earth, liable as it is to corruption and decay — which seems to us either erroneous in conception or irrelevant to the question at issue, or both—arose out of the old Aristotelian philosophy; and in those days a dissertation which neglected points of this kind would have been looked upon probably with contempt, as evading subjects that it ought to have grappled with. The distinction between natural and artificial motion, which occurs repeatedly in the Dialogue, is an instance of an utterly mistaken notion, having its origin in Aristotle, who, great philosopher though he was in other ways, failed in his investigations of physical science, partly from being misled by verbal fallacies.*

Another point that our author endeavours to establish in the first day's dialogue is that the Moon is not a polished surface, as Simplicio and others thought, but much like our own Earth, with mountains and plains and seas—this last being a mistake, as subsequent observation has shown. The solar spots are also discussed, and so, incidentally, is the question whether the heavenly bodies are inhabited, the affirmative opinion finding little favour with any one.

During the second day the great subject is the revolution of the Earth on its axis; and Salviati urges forcibly the improbability of the motion of the whole celestial sphere round the Earth in twenty-four hours, including such a number of vast bodies, and with such an immense velocity, while one single body

* A brief but interesting résumé of the Aristotelian physics is given in Whewell's "History of the Inductive Sciences," a work to which I shall have occasion to refer more than once.

(the Earth), turning round on itself, would produce the same effect. He argues also that if you believe in this motion of the celestial sphere, you must suppose the planets to be moving in two opposite directions at the same time, the diurnal one from east to west, and the annual one from west to east—using the word *annual* in its extended sense, as applied to the periodical revolutions of all the planets. To this Simplicio makes the sapient answer that Aristotle proves that circular motions are not contrary to each other; upon which the third interlocutor, Sagredo, asks him whether when two knights meet one another in the open field, or two fleets at sea — in the latter case sinking each other — such motions can be called contrary? This Simplicio is obliged to admit; he uses, however, another argument, which did not seem so absurd in the then existing state of science, namely, that there may be another sphere beyond that of the stars, and itself starless, to which belongs the property of the diurnal revolution, and that this sphere may carry along with it the inferior spheres, these latter participating in its movement. Ideas such as these were part of the pre-telescopic notions of astronomy. Simplicio's argument is in reply to some powerful reasons drawn from the motions of the planets, the nearer revolving in a shorter, and the more remote in a longer period; it being extremely unlikely that they would be all whirled round the Earth in one day; and also from considerations connected with the stars.

It took a long time to disabuse the human mind of the antiquated opinion that the stars and planets were set in vast movable spheres, as lamps might be set in a large revolving cupola.

One of the objections made at that time against the axial rotation of the Earth was that, if it were really the case, any weight dropped from a high tower would fall some way to the west of the tower, on account of the latter having been carried on eastward by the revolution of the Earth during the few seconds the weight takes in falling,* and that such a result was contrary to experience. In those days, when even the first law of motion had been barely guessed at, the second law, that of the action of combined forces on any body, was of course not generally understood; and a considerable debate as to this point occurs in this same day's dialogue. Simplicio has the hardihood to assert that if a stone be let fall from the mast of a vessel, the vessel being in motion, it falls behind the mast. Salviati, after making a foolish distinction—in accordance, however, with the philosophical ideas then prevalent — between the natural motion of the Earth on its axis, and the artificial motion of the vessel, asks Simplicio if he has

---

* It is said that a weight dropped from the top of a very high tower falls slightly to the *east*, because the velocity of the axial rotation is greater at the summit of the tower than at its foot, and the stone or ball dropped partakes of the motion of the *highest* part of the tower from which it falls; this is perfectly true in theory; and experiments, made not only from the summits of towers but also in mines, tend to confirm it.

ever tried the experiment, which, of course, he had not. He then tells him, and most truly so, that the experiment, if made, would show a very different result, and that the stone would fall at the foot of the mast, whether the vessel were in motion or not. Further on, Simplicio maintained that a projectile thrown from the hand, according to Aristotle's argument, is carried on by the air, itself set in motion by the hand of the projector; and if the stone let fall from the mast of a ship falls at the foot of the mast, it must be the effect of the air. So again he imagines that a ball dropped from the hand of a man, riding fast on horseback, falls some way behind, and does not partake of the horse's speed. Salviati, however, tells him that he deceives himself, and that experience would teach him the contrary.

Various difficulties are discussed in this dialogue well known to the disputants of that day. It being questioned why a projectile shot from a gun point-blank towards the east does not fall above the mark aimed at; or shot westwards fall below it? How it is that birds, when flying, are not left behind by the revolving Earth, since they at any rate are completely detached from the ground above which they are soaring? Why it is that light objects do not fly off at a tangent?

One sees throughout the power of the master-mind of Galileo. He knew many things in mechanics which no subsequent research or experiment has ever corrected; but here and there, as may naturally be supposed, he is at fault. It must ever be remembered that a dialogue, though a convenient form of argument in some respects, does not always give one a clear insight into the author's real convictions. You are not sure whether he quite agrees with any of the spokesmen, and, indeed, Galileo, in his defence before the Inquisition, practically assumes that he did not so agree. It is, however, a good form of discussion for a man whose opinions are intended to be expressed in a *tentative* shape, and perhaps Galileo's mind was in a state congenial to such expression. But, at any rate, it makes it rather more difficult to do justice to the author, as one is never sure what he intends to be taken as the expression of his own deliberate belief; indeed, whatever may have been the amount of indecision in which in this case our author's mind was involved, it is scarcely possible, notwithstanding his disclaimer, to ignore the fact of his strong Copernican opinions.

I think one may say that Galileo did not, at the time when he wrote the dialogue, know the gravity of the air. I say at that time, because it is quite possible that he knew it before his death, since he lived some ten or twelve years after writing this work. It is maintained that he knew it because there is extant a letter from Baliani, the date of which I believe to be about 1631, in which the latter expresses his acknowledgments to Galileo for having taught him this truth. May it not, however, be that what is here meant is the *pressure* of the air? If any one thinks Galileo understood at that time the principle of the gravity of the atmosphere, I refer him to the second day's dialogue. He was aware, no doubt, that the air was carried round by the Earth in its diurnal motion, but why it was so carried round I do not think he quite understood; indeed, as may well be supposed, he did not *clearly* understand what gravity was; it was a mysterious force, drawing heavy bodies towards the centre of the Earth, a force to which we, indeed, give the name of gravity, but of the essence of which we know nothing, as, in fact, we know nothing of the nature of the force that moves the heavenly bodies. This passage is remarkable because it looks as if Galileo half suspected that the force which acted on the Moon and the planets might be akin to that which attracted terrestrial objects towards the centre of the Earth. If he really had arrived at such a conclusion, he would have anticipated the great discovery made thirty or forty years later. I think, however, that he only wished to illustrate the one by the other, and that the allusion means no more. I give, however, the passage in a note,* so that any reader may form his own judgment; and I may add that according to an opinion commonly held by the Copernican school of that age, the adherence of the atmosphere to the Earth as it revolved was the effect of *friction*.

* Simplicio having said that the cause why parts of the earth are carried downwards was gravity, Salviati answers: "Voi errate, Signor Simplicio, voi dovevate dire, che ciaschedun sa, ch' ella si chiama gravità; ma io non vi domando il nome, ma dell' essenza della cosa: della quale essenza voi non sapete punto più di quello,

Our philosopher, wise as he was, had not freed himself from the antiquated notion that some bodies were essentially heavy and others light, which latter had no tendency to descend; not thereby meaning comparatively light substances, but such as were absolutely free from the action of gravity; the fact not being then understood that it is only the resistance of the air that prevents the smallest feather from falling to the ground as quickly as a cannon-shot.

Another mistake into which he falls is that of maintaining, in answer to the argument that the diurnal rotation of the Earth would cause objects to fly off from the surface at a tangent, that *no amount of velocity of rotation* would be sufficient for such a result to follow; whereas, it is well known to modern students of mechanics that if a certain very high velocity of rotation were reached, the centrifugal force would overcome that of gravity, and objects would be projected from the surface of the Earth in the direction of the tangent at that point.

Some irrelevant arguments occur, of which, no

che voi sappiate dell' essenza del movente le Stelle in giro; eccettuatone il nome, che a questa è stato posto, e fatto familiare, e domestico per la frequente esperienza, che mille volte il giorno noi ne veggiamo; ma non è, che realmente noi intentiamo più, che principio, o che virtù sia quella, che muove la pietra in giù, di quel noi sappiamo chi la muova in sù, separata del proiciente; o chi muova la Luna in giro, eccettochè (come ho detto) il nome, che più singolare e proprio gli abbiamo assegnato di gravità; dovechè a quello con termine più generico assegniamo virtù impressa, a quello diamo intelligenza o assistente, o informante; e a infiniti altri moti diamo loro per cagione la natura."

doubt, many were employed at that time on both sides; I think it was the late Professor de Morgan who (in an article written for a popular periodical) made a list of these; and it must in all fairness be said, that this circumstance ought to be taken into account, as palliating the apparent obstinacy of the anti-Copernican party in denying the motion of the Earth. The argument drawn from the tides is, of course, the most striking instance of these scientific fallacies; but it was by no means the only one; in this particular dialogue there is another, which is worth noticing because it confirms what I have just said as to Galileo knowing nothing of the doctrine of universal gravitation. He puts into the mouth of Salviati the argument that bodies which emit light, as do the Sun and fixed stars, are essentially different from those which, like the Earth and planets, have no such property—a distinction which modern astronomy does not endorse—and that, as the Earth in this respect resembles the planets, and the planets are undoubtedly moving, so probably the Earth also is like them in motion, whilst the Sun and the stars remain at rest. It is obvious that ideas of this kind, however plausible they may seem, are utterly at variance with the theory of universal gravitation, according to which, even if the Sun were a dark, cold body and the Earth glowing with heat and light, the Earth would revolve about the Sun just as it does now, *provided the mass of the two bodies remained the same* as at present.

Another suggestion, and a rather amusing one, on the opposition side, was that all things in motion require occasional rest, as we see to be the fact with animals; therefore the Earth, if it were constantly moving, would stand in need of rest—an argument, I suppose, which needs no very elaborate answer.

In the third day's dialogue a question is raised, and sifted at great length, as to whether a certain newly observed star in the constellation Cassiopeia was in the firmament among the distant fixed stars, or "sublunar," *i.e.* nearer to the Earth than the Moon. This star was probably the same as the very remarkable one first observed by Tycho Brahé in 1572, which attained a brilliancy so extraordinary, that it is said to have been equal to the planet Venus, and to have been visible to good eyes in full daylight; in about a month's time it appeared to grow smaller, and gradually faded away until it disappeared entirely —about six months after it was first discovered. This was some years before the invention of the telescope, and the observations were deprived of any assistance they might have gained from that source. The star was one of the most noteworthy of all the variable stars on record.

There followed upon the mention of this star, a dissertation on the method of finding the distances of the heavenly bodies by parallax. The principle of this method was, as we may suppose, well known to Galileo; but he probably did not allow *sufficiently* for the great difficulty in taking accurate observations, especially with the imperfect instruments then in use; I say sufficiently, because that there were such errors he knew, and he insists on the fact in the Dialogue.

Much discourse is spent on the distance of this new star; the apparent reason of which is that it had created some sensation among the astronomers of that day, and therefore the subject received an attention out of proportion to its real importance— I mean importance so far as the Copernican controversy was concerned.

The conversation is then brought back to the objections made by contemporary philosophers to the Copernican system. Aristotle's idea of the universe was that of a vast sphere, or number of concentric hollow spheres, with the Earth in the centre; if that were shown to be probably untrue, his system broke down.* Coming, however, to our own immediate portion of the universe, the question is now raised whether the Earth or the Sun is the centre of revolution. Galileo, by the mouth of Salviati, explains forcibly the argument for the Sun being so. That Mercury and Venus revolve round the Sun he takes for certain; the phases of Venus, which he had

---

* It is curious that the notion of the universe being shaped as a curve returning into itself has been started by some modern German philosophers, founders of what has been called "non-Euclidian geometry." The investigations of astronomers, however, rather point to the conclusion that the stellar universe has no centre, no symmetrical figure, though speculations such as these must always be uncertain.

himself observed, proved it as regards that planet;
and the fact of neither of these bodies ever being
seen far apart from the Sun, greatly strengthened
the conclusion in respect of both of them. A transit
of Mercury over the Sun's disc had, in fact, been
observed in the year 1631, by Gassendi; but Galileo
was doubtless not aware of it when he wrote the
Dialogue.

It being clear then that Venus and Mercury revolve
round the Sun, Galileo shows what strong ground
there is for inferring that the superior planets, Mars,
Jupiter, and Saturn (the others not being then
known), do so also; this he judges from the greater
size of these latter, and particularly of Mars, when in
opposition than when in conjunction; whence we
may conclude that the Earth, which as well as the Sun
is contained within their orbits, is not in the centre of
them, or nearly so. It is remarkable that Galileo
treats all the planets as revolving in *circles*, though
one would think he must at that time have been
aware of Kepler's discovery — that they move in
ellipses. He makes Simplicio grant these last-
mentioned points, which is curious; and he also
explains how the telescope showed phenomena, such
as the phases of Venus, which were unknown to
Copernicus. Simplicio has hitherto had no confidence
in this new instrument, and following in the footsteps
of his friends the Peripatetic philosophers, has supposed the appearances in question to be optical
illusions arising from the lenses used; he will, however,

gladly be corrected if in error. Simplicio's mathematical acquirements are not very great, and it is necessary to explain to him that the areas of circles vary in proportion, not to their diameters simply but to the squares of the diameters, a point which arises in reference to the false judgment formed by the naked eye as to the size of the celestial bodies, an error which is corrected by the telescope. Then to those who made it a difficulty that the Earth should move round the Sun, not alone, but accompanied by the Moon, Salviati is made to reply that Jupiter revolves round the Sun accompanied by four moons.

Again the greater simplicity of the Copernican theory, in accounting for the planetary motions, as they appear to us, is expounded by the same personage.

Galileo occasionally makes the interlocutors allude to himself as "il nostro amico comune," "il nostro Accademico Linceo," etc., and thus claims credit for having been the first to discover the solar spots, a credit which ought not to belong exclusively to him, as Fabricius and the Jesuit Father Scheiner saw the spots at about the same time.

An argument is here attempted to be drawn in favour of the Earth's annual motion from the apparent course of the Sun-spots, and the curves they sometimes describe (as viewed from hence), owing to the inclination of the Sun's axis to an axis perpendicular to the plane of the ecliptic—an inclination of about 7°; there is nothing, however, at all conclusive in such argument, because the appearances in question result from the different *relative* positions of the Earth and Sun at different seasons of the year, and would be the same whichever of the two bodies were in motion.

There follows some conversation arising from one of the anti-Copernican books of that day; one of the difficulties suggested, being the vast distance at which you must suppose the fixed stars to be placed, if Copernicus be right. We who are accustomed to the idea of these immense distances, can scarcely understand the prejudices of the philosophers of that age against admitting them. And it is worth noting that Galileo takes for granted, while answering these theoretical objections, the calculation of his predecessors—that the distance of the Sun is that of 1,208 semi-diameters of the Earth, that is something more than 4,800,000 miles, about one-nineteenth part of what we now know it to be. So also he supposes the size of the Sun to be much less than what is really the case. He was also under the erroneous impression, arising doubtless from the imperfection of the instruments he used, that the stars really had an apparent diameter, though less than Tycho Brahé and other astronomers had supposed, and estimates the angular diameter of a star of the first magnitude at about 5"; consequently he imagined the stars to be much nearer than is actually the fact. It is well known to modern observers, that the apparent size of a star is the effect of an optical illusion, and that greatly as the stars vary in brightness, they present no appreciable diameter at all to the eye; not even those classed as being of the first magnitude.

Another and more weighty objection to Copernicus is, however, urged by the mouth of Simplicio, and it is this—if the Earth really makes an annual revolution round the Sun, why do not the fixed stars, viewed as they must be at different seasons of the year from points so widely distant, change their apparent positions in the heavens? We have just seen that the true distance of the Sun was not known at that time;—if it had been known, and if the men of that age had been aware that the diameter of the Earth's orbit was about 184,000,000 miles in length, the objection would have been still more forcible. But the modern answer to it is conclusive: the stars, or rather a certain number of them, do actually undergo a small displacement in their apparent position every year, or in the technical language of astronomy, they have an annual parallax, a fact which not merely disposes of the objection, but actually confirms the truth of the Copernican theory.

Galileo's reply (by the mouth of Salviati) is to the effect that the followers of Ptolemy admit that it takes 36,000 years to effect a complete revolution of the starry sphere; then, judging from the planets, the length of time required for the orbit is in proportion to the distance, and we suppose the distance of the starry sphere to be, on such assumption, 10,800 semi-diameters of the Earth's orbit (or Sun's orbit, as they called it). At so great a distance as that, the change of position caused by the Earth's annual motion round the Sun would not be appreciable.

The principle of this reply is of course quite sound, and we, who know the stars to be considerably farther from us than the above estimate supposes, can well understand that the vast majority of them have no annual parallax whatever, that the finest instruments can discover.

To further objections drawn from the enormous distances of the stars, and the difficulty of perceiving the use which such remote bodies can be to the Earth, it is replied that such speculations are useless and presumptuous, and also that words like small, very small, immense, etc., are relative rather than absolute.

Some pains are taken in the course of the dialogue to explain how the stars, according to their different positions, would be affected by annual parallax, supposing such to be discoverable, and assuming the motion of the Earth. And a minute explanation is also given, on this latter assumption, of the length of day and night varying in different latitudes according to the seasons; illustrating the fact that details which appear to us elementary and are taught to schoolboys, were strange to the minds even of educated and learned men in those days.

One remark, arising from the questions connected with stellar parallax, is most striking, as showing how far Galileo was advanced in his knowledge of pure mathematics as well as of mechanics and astronomy. Salviati is made to say that the circumference of an infinite circle is identical with a straight line: "sono l' istessa cosa." This idea, familiar though it be to modern mathematicians, is one that we should not have expected to find enunciated in the early part of the seventeenth century; even the intelligent Sagredo cannot understand or believe it, and it is not further discussed; but the fact of its being here stated is especially noteworthy.*

Another (less felicitous) guess is hazarded by the same interlocutor Salviati, who, as I have already remarked, appears to be the one that most nearly represents the author's own mind,—to account for the Earth keeping her axis pointed (approximately, that is to say) in the same direction during each annual revolution round the Sun. Salviati suggests that it may be due to some magnetic influence, and that the interior of the Earth may be a vast loadstone. This is strange, because it is evident from what immediately preceded, that the author was aware of the true reason, which in fact he illustrates by the well-known experiment of a light ball floating in a bucket of water, to which a revolving motion is imparted. It seems, however, that a work by William Gilbert on the subject of

* To speak of the circumference of a circle of infinite radius as being identical with a straight line (though practically true enough) is not rigidly accurate. We should say that they approximate infinitely to one another, or in mathematical phraseology, they are equal to each other *in the limit*.

magnetism had had some influence on the scientific
thought of the period, and that Galileo had considered it worthy of his attention. The writer had
maintained the probability of this theory, of the
Earth's interior being an enormous loadstone—not
an unnatural idea in the then-existing state of
science—and Galileo was evidently somewhat fas-
cinated by the hypothesis. Magnetism was attracting the notice of the philosophers of that day, and
the property of the needle, which is termed the *dip*,
had been recently discovered.

There is not much else worthy of special mention
in the third day's dialogue; which in fact, as a whole,
is not equal to that of the second day.

The fourth day is mainly devoted to the argument
drawn from the tides. It was in handling this branch
of the subject that Galileo's great sagacity and power
of discernment seem to have deserted him. It is a
curious thing that the inhabitant of a Mediterranean
country, who, for all that one knows, never saw a
really great tide in his life, should have seized upon
this topic, and so utterly misused and perverted it.

If, instead of living in Italy, he had resided at an
English seaport, he would probably have never fallen
into the mistakes he thus made. In the Mediterranean
there are currents, arising from other causes, which he,
however, attributed to tidal action; but for the most
part there is little, if any, appreciable ebb and flow of
the tides, scarcely any perceptible rise and fall of the
sea, a fact which he particularly notices. But in some

few places, and notably at Venice, there is a sensible tide, so it is said, causing a difference of a few feet between high and low water.

Now Galileo was under the impression that the ebb and flow took each about six hours, following the ordinary solar day; whereas, if he had observed the phenomenon on the shores of any sea, where the tidal wave of the ocean made its full force to be felt, or again, at the mouth of a great tidal river, he never could have failed to perceive that the rise and fall of the water follow approximately the *lunar*, and not the solar day, the former being fifty minutes longer than the latter. It must of course be understood that the theory of the tides was first investigated fully and scientifically by the same great genius to whom we owe the theory of universal gravitation; and Galileo, who lived half a century earlier, may well be excused for not having grasped it. But it had long been known that the Sun and Moon had an influence upon the tides, and as I have just stated, any one who watched the movements of the sea from day to day, and from week to week, at a place where there is a great rise and fall—as for instance, in the Bristol Channel—could not fail to perceive that the Moon had the principal share in the work, however unable he might be to comprehend the theory. Besides which, the theory, however obvious to us (at least in its main outlines), was not by any means so intelligible to the men of Galileo's age. They might just guess that the Sun exercised some attractive influence over the Earth, and the Earth again over the Moon, but they did not know that the Moon attracted the Earth exactly in the same way, though with far inferior potency, owing to her much smaller mass; and consequently they were not aware of the Moon's power to raise the great tidal wave in the ocean, to which are due the remarkable phenomena so familiar to the inhabitants of the English coasts.

Galileo would have been wise if he had not touched on a point which he neither understood in theory, nor had properly acquainted himself with by practical observation. Good causes are often damaged by bad arguments, and such was the case on this occasion.* There was, however, something ingenious in his argument. If you take a basin of water, and move it along quite smoothly and evenly, no great commotion in the water takes place; but suppose some stoppage or jerk to occur, the result will be, as we know, very different. Now the Earth has two motions, one round its axis in twenty-four hours, and the other round the Sun in one year; every point, then, on the Earth's surface moves through space more rapidly while on that side of the globe which is turned away

---

* It is not intended here to deny what some writers state—that the *friction* caused by the Earth's rotation does in some degree act upon the tidal wave. It is remarkable, so far as can be ascertained from observations taken at some small island at a distance from any continent, that the tidal wave of the Ocean only rises, even at the spring, about five or six feet. The enormous rise of water at some places arises from the tidal wave being driven into estuaries, mouths of rivers, and other narrow channels.

from the Sun, than on that side which by the diurnal revolution is turned round in the contrary direction. Here, then, with the sea lying in its vast basin, and revolving with other things on the surface of the Earth from west to east every day, and thus accelerated in its motion through space during twelve hours and retarded during the other twelve hours, you have on a large scale the same result that a basin, half full of water, held in your hands and checked by some retarding obstacle, gives you on a very small and minute scale. Strange indeed it is that a man who was acquainted with the laws of motion sufficiently to know that anything thrown or dropped in a vessel or a vehicle, partook of the motion of the latter and followed its course (so long as it remained within the vehicle) just as if the whole were at rest—that he should have failed to perceive that the ocean, lying in its bed in that mighty vehicle the Earth, would be carried round in the daily rotation with an uniform velocity, unless interfered with by the attraction of other bodies. Simplicio, who for once is right, puts the difficulty, that if the sea behaved in the way supposed, the air would do so in the same way: the reply to which is that the air being thin and light is less adherent to the Earth than the water which is heavier, and does not accommodate itself to the Earth's movements as water does; further, that where the air is not hemmed in, as it were, by mountains and other inequalities on the Earth's surface, it really is partially left behind by the diurnal rotation, and in the neighbourhood of the tropics, where the effect is chiefly felt, a constant wind blows accordingly from east to west. Our philosopher had evidently heard of the trade winds, though he had not acquired an accurate knowledge of their course or of their origin. It is undoubtedly true that they do help strongly to prove the revolution of the Earth, because they arise from cold currents of air flowing in from the north and from the south respectively towards the tropics, to supply the place of the atmosphere rarefied by the sun's heat, and consequently ascending, as is the case in those regions. Then these cold currents, coming from latitudes where there is a less velocity of rotation, tend to preserve that velocity and lag behind the Earth as it revolves, so that they have the effect of north-easterly winds in the northern hemisphere, and south-easterly in the southern hemisphere. Galileo's imperfect information prevented him from using this important argument.

However, to return to the tides. He had to account for other phenomena, besides the daily rise and fall, namely, for the much greater rise and fall which take place soon after new and full moon, and which are known as the spring-tides. Unable to deny that these were in some way due to lunar influence, he took refuge in the supposition that the Moon, when at the full, retarded the motion of the Earth in its orbit, since as the two travel together round the Sun at those particular times, they form, as it were, a lengthened pendulum, longer than at other times by the semi-diameter of the lunar orbit; and therefore (like any other pendulum) must vibrate more slowly. I should say that he does not appear to have been aware of the existence of *two* spring-tides in each lunation, and therefore only tries to account for one ; and it is obvious that this method of explaining them is not only utterly inadequate, but even absurd. The Moon truly enough exercises a certain disturbing influence on the orbital motion of the Earth, but that has nothing to do with the spring-tides.

There remained the necessity of accounting for the annual, or, more properly, semi-annual increase of the ebb and flow of the sea. Galileo suggests that this arises from the angle made by the plane of the equator with the ecliptic at the equinoxes, owing to which there would not be the same counteraction exercised by the Earth's motion in its orbit on the waters of the ocean at those periods as there would at the solstices. But it seems that this would rather tend to diminish the tides than to increase them, as, indeed, would be the case as regards the last-mentioned explanation with respect to the ordinary spring-tides. What really does happen at the equinoxes is, that the Sun and the full or new Moon being at those times vertical to the equator (or nearly so), they have a greater attractive force than at other spring-tides over the vast expanse of the ocean, and the tides are consequently greater. There is also another increase which sometimes occurs when the

Moon happens to be at its least distance from the Earth at the time of spring-tides, but that was unknown to Galileo. He touches, however, and very properly so, on the great modifications in the tides caused by various gulfs, by the forms of the great continents, and the shapes of different seas—modifications, in fact, which are well known to be almost innumerable, and have been learnt only by careful observation and experience.

One of the worst features of this Dialogue is the contempt which the author shows for those opinions on the subject which differ from his own; and it is difficult to suppress a feeling of disgust when he alludes in this way to Kepler, who had partly guessed the true cause of the tides, and of whom he otherwise speaks in terms of respect.*

If a man of science, when he wishes to publish to the world a discovery or a hypothesis, adopts the form of a dialogue as a method of stating his case, he ought in all reason to do full justice to the antagonistic side, and state his opponent's case as well as his own. I fear that Galileo failed to do this, not only in this particular dialogue, but also to some extent in those of the three preceding days. Sim-

---

* These are the author's words, spoken by Salviati: "Tra tutti gli nomini grandi, che sopra tal mirabile effetto di natura hanno filosofato, più mi maraviglio del Keplero, che di altri, il quale d' ingegno libero, e acuto, e che aveva in mano i moti attribuiti alla terra, abbia poi dato l' orecchio, e assenso a *predominii della Luna sopra l' acqua*, e a proprietà occulte, e simili fanciullezze."

plicio, as I said above, is not a fool, but as a personage in a scientific argument he is lamentably deficient.

Simplicio at the end of the Dialogue urges that God could, in His infinite power, cause the tides by some other means than those suggested by Salviati, to which true and pious (though, perhaps, rather irrelevant) argument the latter respectfully and devoutly assents.

The concluding sentences are said, as I have remarked elsewhere, to have been recast or retouched by Father Riccardi.

It is worth noticing that there is a passage in the fourth day's dialogue, in which the author alludes to the fact of the Sun being apparently longer by about nine days in passing along the ecliptic from the spring to the autumn equinox, than in passing from the autumnal to the vernal; that is to say, of the northern hemisphere having so much longer summer than winter, and he treats it as one of the recondite problems of astronomy not as yet understood. This is an additional proof that for some reason or another he had not made himself acquainted with Kepler's researches; for as soon as it became known that the planets move, not in circles, but in ellipses, with the Sun in one of the foci, it was obvious that there would be in every case (though in some more than others) this inequality to which allusion has been made, and the Earth, if a planet, would be subject to the same rule as the rest.

Such, then, is a somewhat imperfect *précis* of this famous work of Galileo, which owes its importance to the historical circumstances connected with its publication quite as much, to say the least of it, as to its own intrinsic merit.

CHAPTER IV.

RESUMING the history of events, we find that early in the year 1632 the printing of the Dialogue was completed. The author caused some copies to be bound and gilt and sent to Rome. It was not easy to pass them, on account of the quarantine; yet some amongst them found their way, and great was the sensation caused in the ecclesiastical world by their appearance.

There were a few admirers of Galileo who approved warmly; but there was the School of Aristotle, as in these enlightened days there is the School of Darwin,[*] and they could not bear that anything should be published reflecting on the scientific infallibility of their great philosopher. Thus we find that Father Scheiner, writing to Gassendi, observed that Galileo had written his work " contra communem Peripateticorum Scholam."

The agitation against the book was successful, and a report arose forthwith that it would be condemned. The report was no mere *canard*, as the subsequent

[*] It is not intended to imply that these two Schools of thought stand on anything like the same scientific level.

proceedings soon showed. In the month of August of this same year the Master of the Sacred Palace gave orders to the printer at Florence to suspend the distribution of the copies, and he also sent for those which had been brought to Rome. Nor was this all. In the following month the Pope ordered that a letter should be written to the Inquisitor of Florence, enjoining him to direct Galileo to present himself in Rome in the month of October, in order to explain his conduct.

The book had already been examined by special Commission—a step taken with the view of pleasing the Grand Duke of Tuscany, so as to avoid bringing the affair before the Inquisition.

The Pope, from whatever cause, was much displeased. This appeared in a conversation with Niccolini, the Tuscan Ambassador, in which His Holiness said that Galileo had entered on ground which he ought not to have touched, and that both Ciampoli and the Master of the Sacred Palace had been deceived. Still it seemed that, so far, there was no intention to do more than censure the book and demand a retractation.

The special Commission, of which mention has just been made, after a month's interval, reported that Galileo had been disobedient to orders in the following respects: Affirming as an absolute truth the movement of the Earth instead of stating it as a hypothesis; attributing the tides to this cause—*i.e.* to the revolution and movement of the Earth; deceitfully keeping silence as to the order given him in 1616 to abandon the opinion that the Earth revolved, and that the Sun was the centre of the universe.

Another memorial (drawn up about the same time), after enumerating the facts of the case, stated eight heads of accusation against the philosopher:

1.—Having, without leave, placed at the beginning of his work the permission for printing, delivered at Rome.
2.—Having, in the body of the work, put the true doctrine in the mouth of a fool, and having approved it but feebly by the argument of another interlocutor.
3.—Having quitted the region of hypothesis by affirming, in an absolute manner, the mobility of the Earth and the stability of the Sun, etc.
4.—Having treated the subject as one that was not already decided, and in the attitude of a person waiting for a definition, and supposing it to have not been yet promulgated.
5.—Having despised the authors who were opposed to the above-mentioned opinion, though the Church uses them in preference to others.
6.—Having affirmed (untruly) the equality supposed to exist, for understanding geometrical matters, between the divine and human intellect.
7.—Having stated, as a truth, that the partisans of Ptolemy ought to range themselves with those of Copernicus, and denied the converse.

8.—Having wrongly attributed the tides to the stability of the Sun and mobility of the Earth, which things do not exist.

It must be observed that all this was merely of the nature of an accusation, and was in no way an ecclesiastical decision.

It appears, too, that some apprehensions were entertained in Rome that false philosophical and theological doctrines might be drawn out of the opinion put forth by Galileo. No. 6 of the above-mentioned accusations points in that direction.

At any rate, no time was lost in summoning the philosopher to Rome, there to answer for his offences. A message to that effect was communicated to him by the Inquisitor at Florence, on the 1st October. Upon this, Galileo, anxious to gain time, and to excuse himself from going to Rome, if it were possible to do so, wrote to Cardinal Barberini, and sought the powerful advocacy of the Grand Duke of Tuscany; he urged his infirm health, and advanced age, nearly seventy years, as grounds for consideration. It was intimated to him, however, that although some little time would be allowed him on the ground of health, yet to Rome he must come; and a threat was added, through the Inquisitor at Florence, of bringing him fettered as a prisoner if it turned out that his health was not really such as he represented it to be. So at last he yielded, and started for Rome on the 20th January, 1633, and, travelling very slowly, arrived on the 13th February, when the Tuscan Ambassador, Niccolini, who had sent his litter for him, received him at his Palace. This, with all the freedom it implied, was indeed an unusual indulgence to persons situated as he was. After a short time, during which no official steps were taken, he was conveyed to the office of the Inquisition, and lodged there, but well and commodiously, by the Pope's order.

On the 12th April he appeared for the first time before the Court; he admitted the authorship of the Dialogue; he admitted, too, that the decree of the Index had been notified to him; but stated that Cardinal Bellarmine had informed him that it was allowable to hold the Copernican doctrine as a hypothesis. He maintained further that he had not contravened the order given him, that he should not defend or support this doctrine; and he declared that he did not remember having been forbidden in any way to teach it.

It would seem that this latter prohibition was meant to include teaching by implication, such as one may do through the medium of an interlocutor in a dialogue.

It is startling that Galileo should have said among other things on this occasion, that he had not embraced or defended in his book the opinion that the Earth is in motion and the Sun stationary; but, on the contrary, had shown that the reasons produced by Copernicus were feeble and inconclusive.

After this examination he was well lodged, though

treated as a prisoner, being placed in the apartments of the "Fiscal of the Holy Office," instead of in the ordinary chambers appropriated to accused persons; moreover, he had leave to walk in the garden, and was attended by his own servant. He said himself, in a letter to his friend Bocchineri, that his health was good, and that he had every attention shown to him by the Tuscan Ambassador and Ambassadress. It is well to note these things, because they dispose of the popular accusations of cruelty which have been made by ignorant or malicious controversialists, although the antagonists with whom I am dealing are too well informed to resort to them.

A slight indisposition from which our philosopher suffered about this time, illustrated still further the desire which existed to treat him with *personal* kindness; the Commissary and the Fiscal charged with the process, both visited him and spoke encouragingly to him. As soon as he had recovered he requested to have a further hearing. This took place on the 30th April; but meanwhile, three theologians, who had been consulted, Augustin Orezzi, Melchior Inchofer, and Zacharias Pasqualigo, had each separately presented a memorial to the effect that Galileo had taught in his book the motion of the Earth and the immobility of the Sun. At the hearing on the 30th April, being asked to say whatever occurred to him, he stated that he had read his Dialogue again—not having seen it for three years previously—in order to ascertain if there was anything—"se contro alla mia purissima intenzione, per mia inavertenza"—by which he had been at all disobedient to the order imposed on him in 1616; and he had found there were some arguments, notably about the solar spots and the tides, which he had put too forcibly, and which he thought could be refuted. As regards the latter of these two points we may, I think, cordially agree with him in his retractation; but it had been a favourite argument with him. He also stated on this occasion—not having, I fear, the courage of his convictions—that he had not held as true the condemned opinion as to the Earth's motion, and was ready to write something fresh in order to refute it, if the time to do so were allowed him.

On this same day (30th April) the Commissary-General of the Inquisition, with the Pope's sanction, allowed Galileo to be imprisoned, under certain conditions, at the Palace of the Tuscan Ambassador, this favour being conceded on account of his age and health.

He was again called before the Court on the 10th May, and he then presented a written statement, to which was appended the original of Cardinal Bellarmine's injunction, laid on him in 1616. It contained certain prohibitions, but not the word "teach."

He pleaded also that he had done his best to avoid all fault in his book, which he had himself submitted to the Grand Inquisitor. Now follows what seems like more severe treatment, whether because he had not impressed his judges with a belief in his candour and sincerity, or from other reasons. However, the Pope, on the 16th June, gave orders that he should be questioned as to his *intention*; then, after he had been *threatened* with torture (apparently without any view of putting the threat into execution), and made to pronounce an abjuration full and entire, that he should be condemned to prison according to the discretion of the Inquisition; also that his treatise should be prohibited, and himself forbidden to treat, either by word or writing, on the subject of the Sun and the Earth.

Yet, with all this, the Pope, two days afterwards, said to Niccolini, the Tuscan Ambassador, that it was impossible not to prohibit this opinion (Copernicanism) as it was contrary to the Holy Scriptures, and that Galileo must remain a prisoner for some time for having contravened the orders given him in 1616, but that he (the Pope) would see if the condemnation could be mitigated.

It appears that he was thinking of sentencing him to a temporary seclusion in the Monastery of Santa Croce, at Florence.

When, in pursuance of the Pope's order, Galileo was questioned (21st June), he was asked how long it was since he had held the opinion that the Sun, and not the Earth, was the centre of the universe; to which he replied that long before the decree of 1616 he held that the two opinions could equally be sustained; but that since the decree, convinced as he was of the prudence of the superior authorities, all uncertainty in his mind had ceased, that he had then adopted, and still held, the opinion of Ptolemy on the mobility of the Sun as true and indubitable. Certain passages in his book were then put to him as being irreconcilable with the statements he was making; and yet he maintained that, though he had stated the case *pro* and *con* in his work, he did not, in his heart, hold the condemned opinion. "Concludo dunque dentro di me medesimo ne tenere ne haver tenuto dopo la determinazione delli Superiori la dannata opinione."

Threatened with torture if he did not tell the truth, he persevered in his answer as already given; upon which the tribunal, after making him sign his deposition, dismissed him. On the next day, the 22nd June, he was taken to Santa Maria Sopra Minerva, and brought before the Cardinals and Prelates of the Congregation, that he might hear his sentence and pronounce his abjuration.

The accusation was that he had openly violated the order given him not to maintain Copernicanism; that he had unfairly extorted permission to print his book, without showing the prohibition received in 1616; that he had maintained the condemned opinion, although he alleged that he had left it undecided and as simply probable—which, however, was still a grave error, since an opinion declared contrary to Scripture could not in any way be probable.

His sentence was to the effect that he had rendered

himself strongly suspected of heresy in believing and maintaining a doctrine false and opposed to Holy Scripture in respect of the motion of the Sun and the Earth, and in believing that one might maintain and defend any opinion after it had been declared to be contrary to Holy Scripture. He had, therefore, incurred the censures in force against those who offend in such ways; from which, however, he would be absolved provided that, with a sincere heart and unfeigned faith, he would abjure the said errors and heresies; but, as a penance and as a warning to others, he was to undergo certain inflictions. The book was henceforth to be prohibited, he himself was to be condemned to the ordinary prison of the Holy Office for a time the Holy Office would itself limit, and he was to recite the seven Penitential Psalms once a week for three years. The Holy Office reserved to itself the power to remit or change part or all of the above-named penances. Galileo abjured, accordingly, as directed.

The well-known legend that after his abjuration he stamped on the ground with his foot, saying: "E pur si muove" (And yet it, *i.e.* the Earth, *does* move), is not found in any contemporary author, and first appears towards the end of the eighteenth century. It is also to the last degree improbable; Galileo was in far too great dread of his judges to provoke them by openly perpetrating such an action; and if he did it *sotto voce*, who heard it, and who testified to it? The late Dr. Whewell in his "History of the Inductive Sciences," suggests that it was "uttered as a playful epigram in the ear of a Cardinal's secretary, with a full knowledge that it would be immediately repeated to his master." This writer is eminently fair, though naturally he writes from a Protestant point of view; but he takes the extraordinary line of maintaining what I think no one who knows all the facts could possibly suppose, namely, that the whole thing was a kind of solemn farce, and that the Inquisitors did not believe Galileo's abjuration to be sincere, or even wish it to be so; thus he says: "though we may acquit the Popes and Cardinals of Galileo's time of stupidity and perverseness in rejecting manifest scientific truths, I do not see how we can acquit them of dissimulation and duplicity." That is, he thinks the process was a piece of decorous solemnity, adopted to hoodwink the ecclesiastical public. I do not think it necessary to discuss so improbable a theory. And the story of "E pur si muove," as also that of bodily torture or any personal cruelty being inflicted on Galileo, may, I venture to think, be dismissed into the realm of fable.

The Pope, without delay, commuted the sentence of imprisonment to one of seclusion in the Palace of the Tuscan Ambassador, on the Monte Pincio, after which Galileo was allowed to retire to Sienna, to the Palace of the Archbishop of that place, Piccolomini, one of his warmest friends, from whom he received every possible attention. Indeed, the

Archbishop seems to have gone beyond the limits of prudence, considering the peculiar circumstances of the case and the temper of the times, in the enthusiasm of his admiration for the great astronomer, and to have hinted to various persons that, in his opinion, he had been unjustly condemned, that he was the greatest man in the world and would always live in his writings, even those that had been prohibited; such, at least, was the report that found its way to Rome, and it caused great prejudice to Galileo. He had received permission to go to his country house at Arcetri, near Florence, on condition that he lived there quietly, receiving only the visits of his friends and relatives, in such a way as not to give umbrage; and the report, to which allusion has just been made, coupled with the accusation that, under the encouragement of his host the Archbishop, he had spread opinions that were not soundly Catholic in the city of Sienna, caused some additional strictness to be enforced as to the manner of his seclusion.

Thus he was detained for four years in his villa, and was refused permission to go to Florence for medical treatment, it being, however, apparent that the villa was sufficiently near to the city to enable physicians and surgeons to go *to him* when required. Later on, in 1638, when his sufferings had increased, and he had become (wholly or partially) blind, permission was given him to reside in Florence, on condition that he should not speak to his visitors on the subject of the movement of the Earth. Of this concession he availed himself, and lived for his few remaining years in Florence, occupying himself with scientific pursuits. In this same year he published at Leyden a work entitled, "Dialoghi delle Nuove Scienze"; this, in fact, was his last work of importance, and he died on the 8th January, 1642, in his seventy-eighth year.

It is not easy to form an accurate estimate of the character of Galileo, so far, at least, as affected by the proceedings just related. By some he has been called a "Martyr of Science"; but a martyr, unless the word be used in a loose and inaccurate sense, ought, above all things, to have the courage of his convictions, and as we have seen, that was hardly the case with Galileo. I will here again quote Dr. Whewell's work on the "History of the Inductive Sciences," and this time in agreement with his words: "I do not see with what propriety Galileo can be looked upon as a martyr of science. Undoubtedly he was very desirous of promoting what he conceived to be the cause of philosophical truth; but it would seem that, while he was restless and eager in urging his opinions, he was always ready to make such submissions as the spiritual tribunals required. . . . But in this case (*i.e.* the case of his refusing to abjure) he would have been a martyr to a cause of which the merit was of a mingled character; for his own special and favourite share in the reasonings by which the Copernican system was supported, was the argument drawn from the flux and reflux of the sea, which argument is altogether false."

Yet though we deny him the credit of having been a hero or a martyr, we must not be too severe in condemning him. He was old and enfeebled by bad health; moreover, his friends had advised him to submit fully and unreservedly to the tribunal of the Inquisition. And to this we may add the following considerations. There can be little doubt that he held the Copernican theory as a very probable opinion; how, indeed, with his knowledge of astronomy, and with his own discoveries before his eyes, could it be otherwise? But it is very possible that he had no fixed, absolute conviction on the subject; he was a sincere Catholic, and had a deep respect for the Pope and for the Church, and, unlike modern scientific men, he probably allowed some weight to the decisions of ecclesiastical authorities. Remembering all this, we may well admit that there is much to palliate his conduct, though not fully to justify it.

But his want of candour evidently prejudiced his judges against him. They accepted his reiterated denials of belief, even a qualified belief, in Copernicanism, but they did not credit them as being true. I incline to hold that he would have done as well and given more satisfaction to the tribunal if he had made a straightforward defence in some such way as this: that he could not help believing

Copernicanism to be a probable hypothesis on purely scientific grounds, and *more than this*, the then-existing state of astronomical knowledge would not have justified him in saying: that he left to the ecclesiastical authorities henceforth the entire question of reconciling the theory with Holy Scripture, and that he would not in future teach it even as a hypothesis, or publish any work so teaching it, without permission. A statement of this nature, coupled with an apology for any indiscretion connected with the publication of the Dialogue, might have availed him better than the line he adopted, and would at least have had the merit of candour.

A few words may here be added on the scientific character of Galileo; in this respect he was, with the exception of Kepler, the first man of his age.

He has the credit of being the discoverer of the first law of motion; but whether he fully realised this all-important law, or whether it was one of those happy guesses which we sometimes find to have been made by men who are the precursors of great discoverers, but who do not perceive the full scope and the ultimate bearing of the truths on which they have lighted, I need not here discuss. He did, however, state the law in a Dialogue on mechanics, published in 1638, in these words:

" I imagine a movable body projected in a horizontal plane, all impediments [to motion] being removed; it is then manifest from what has been said more fully elsewhere, that its (the body's) motion will be uniform and perpetual upon the plane, if the plane be extended to infinity."

This of course involves the principle of the first of the three laws of motion, the Newtonian laws, as they are frequently called, because the man whose name they bear was the one who used them clearly and consistently as the basis of a great astronomical theory. The law, as now usually stated, is fuller and more explicit than that given by Galileo, and may be enunciated thus: "Every body perseveres in its state of rest, or of uniform motion in a straight line, unless it is compelled to change that state by forces impressed on it."

It is, however, greatly to the scientific credit of Galileo that before the close of his life he should have emancipated himself from the erroneous idea that circular motion alone is naturally uniform, and should have stated in the language just quoted the true mechanical doctrine, unknown to his predecessors, unknown even to Kepler, a doctrine which involved nothing less than a revolution in the conception of the laws of motion. Nor was this his only contribution to the science of mechanics; he it was who first understood the law that regulates the velocity of falling bodies; he perceived that they were acted upon by an uniformly accelerating force, that of terrestrial gravity, and that the velocity at any given point is proportional to the time of descent.

The principle of virtual velocities is said by some

persons to have been discovered by Galileo, and it appears that he stated it fully and clearly; but he can scarcely be said to be the discoverer of it, as it had been known to others, and had even—at least as exemplified in the case of the lever—been noticed by Aristotle. There is, however, no doubt that Galileo was the greatest man of his day in mechanical knowledge, whether we attribute more or less weight to the light he threw on particular details.

In astronomy he was necessarily a discoverer, for the all-important reason that, as already stated, he was the first man that ever used the telescope for investigating the phenomena of the heavens. He thus saw what no one previously had seen,* the satellites of Jupiter, the spots on the Sun, and the moon-like phases of the planet Venus, besides the greatly increased number of stars, so many of which are invisible to the naked eye.

The first-mentioned of these discoveries, that of the satellites of Jupiter, seems to have created an immense sensation among the *savants* of that day. It *suggested* that the theories of Ptolemy were anything but complete or correct, and yet it *proved* nothing, excepting against those *à priori* reasoners, who would not believe that a body round which a moon circulated could itself be in motion; but the phases of Venus were simply conclusive against the

---

* The spots on the Sun were seen at about the same period of time by Fabricius and by Father Scheiner, a Jesuit, as already mentioned.

Ptolemaic system, and for this reason: According to
that system Venus was a planet revolving round the
Earth in an orbit outside that of Mercury, but within
that of the Sun. Now the phases of Venus did not
correspond with any supposed period of her revolution round the Earth, as the phases of the Moon
obviously do, nor did any one ever imagine that the
Earth went round Venus. They did, however, correspond with the time of a probable orbit in which
either Venus revolved round the Sun or the Sun
round Venus; and here again this latter alternative
was inadmissible. There remained, therefore, the
one only reasonable solution of the phenomenon,
namely, that Venus travelled in an orbit round the
Sun. This was further confirmed when, in December,
1639, our own countryman, Horrox, at that time a
young curate residing in the north of England, but
gifted with a knowledge of astronomy which would
have done credit to a man of double his age and
experience, observed a transit of the planet across
the Sun's disc. This occurred some few years after
Galileo's condemnation; but it may be remarked that
Gassendi had already, in November, 1631, witnessed
a transit of Mercury. Thùs it appeared that these
two planets revolved round the Sun, contrary to what
Ptolemy had supposed. And yet this was not conclusive in favour of Copernicanism, for the theory
of Tycho Brahé was precisely to this effect: that
the planets revolved round the Sun, and that the Sun
in his turn circulated round the Earth. This hypo-

thesis was of the nature of a compromise, and it has been said that Tycho was led to it by his interpretation of Scripture rather than of Nature; yet he was one of the best astronomers and best observers of his age, and had Kepler for one of his pupils. He had a reason, too, for rejecting Copernicanism which in his time seemed to have considerable weight, namely, the incredible distances at which the fixed stars must be supposed to be placed if the theory were true, since no sensible motion could be detected among them—apparent motion, that is—such as would result from the annual motion of the Earth if the stars were at any distance approaching to that of the planets. We know now how futile this objection is, but in that age there was an idea that Nature could never allow of such a waste of space as is implied in these vast distances. If Tycho had lived longer, we may well doubt whether he would have adhered to his system. Kepler saw its weakness, and was the first to discover the true nature of the curves which both the Earth and the planets describe in their respective orbits; and this, although he did not know the first law of motion. His books, published in 1619 and 1622, stated not only the elliptic form of the orbits, which no one previously had found out, but also the important law connecting the distances of the planets with their periods of revolution.

It is necessary to bear in mind how gradually these various items of knowledge dawned upon the scientific world, and how imperfect was the state in which the study of astronomy remained until the discovery of that great law of gravitation, which binds together and regulates the physical universe. Men of mature years had not then learnt the lesson now taught to youths at college, that in natural science we must discard *à priori* arguments, and trust to the experimental method for guidance. It has been said contemptuously that the Cardinals who condemned Galileo and the Copernican system were not only ignorant of the science of the present day (which was inevitable), but even of that of their own day. If that means merely that they were deficient in that far-reaching intelligence which enables some gifted men to foresee the future effect of recent discoveries and hypotheses scarcely emerged from a state of embryo, we may readily grant it.

We may allow also that some of the recent discoveries of Galileo, as, for instance, that of the phases of Venus, were not at first fully appreciated, nor their bearing on the controversy perfectly understood, excepting by professed astronomers. It required careful observation to perceive that this planet's phases were only to be explained on the theory of her revolving round the Sun.

On the other hand, if these ecclesiastics were wise enough to see the futility of Galileo's argument drawn from the tides, it is certainly not for us to blame them; the tides have nothing to do with the questions then at issue.

And it is only fair to remember that supposing

Ptolemy completely overthrown, as in reality he assuredly was, by the observations on Venus and Mercury, there remained the system of Tycho Brahé, as has been remarked already, and this system partly met the case of those phenomena that Ptolemy failed in accounting for; and although we can easily see now that it was something of the nature of a makeshift, at that time there was no clear or conclusive evidence against it.

I proceed now to state what appears to have been the ecclesiastical force of the two condemnations by the Roman tribunals—that of the Index prohibiting certain books, and that of the Inquisition punishing Galileo individually, and forcing him to abjure his real or imputed opinions on the Copernican system of astronomy. I trust I shall not lose sight of my position as a *lay theologian* (in the sense I have defined the term), or trespass upon strictly ecclesiastical preserves; but I may surely say at once, that it is evident no decision was pronounced on any matter of faith. The first case, that of the Index in 1616, I have already discussed; and as for the latter one, that of the Inquisition, it seems hardly credible that any one should maintain that the sentence of a Roman tribunal on an individual, however eminent, could constitute an *ex cathedrâ* decision on a question of faith. Mr. Roberts, however, seems to maintain something very like this; but he does so by taking some strong, and perhaps extreme, statements made by theologians, such as M. Bouix and Dr. Ward, when writing on some totally different point, and by urging that if these things are true, then Galileo's condemnation was tantamount to a definition *de fide*.

I do not feel called upon to answer arguments of this kind. But there is another which is more relevant, drawn from the Brief addressed by Pope Pius IX. to the Archbishop of Munich, about twenty-five years ago, when the congress of philosophers, of whom Dr. Döllinger was the leading spirit, had been held in that city. In that Brief, the Pope states that it is requisite for good Christians to subject themselves in conscience to decisions pertaining to doctrine that are put forth by the Pontifical Congregations; and also to such heads of doctrine as are held to be theological truths by the common consent of Catholics, even when the denial of these does not involve heresy, but deserves some other censure.

Theologians, I believe, are not agreed as to whether this Brief is strictly *ex cathedrâ*, and therefore to be treated as infallible. But let us assume that it is so. Does the expression, " subject themselves in conscience," mean necessarily anything more than a respectful acquiescence, as distinguished from a full interior assent? And, allowing that it does even mean this latter, it is for *doctrinal* decisions that such authority is claimed; and what I am maintaining is, that the decrees in the case of Galileo were purely disciplinary.

I do not of course deny that the line of demarcation between doctrinal and disciplinary is sometimes hard to define. But surely the putting of books on the "Index Librorum Prohibitorum," whatever be the reasons stated for doing so, is essentially an act of discipline; and so also is the condemnation of any individual man for having disobeyed injunctions laid upon him by authority, or for having disregarded the principles laid down by the same authority for the regulation of its practical conduct, so long as they were in force, and not repealed by any subsequent act.

And this leads me to touch upon another argument of Mr. Roberts, who says, truly enough, that the authority of Rome is greater than that of individual theologians, and that Rome must know her own mind. And because the decision of the Inquisition in 1633, condemning Galileo personally, referred in strong and marked language to the decree of the Index in 1616, therefore he infers that the latter is thereby proved to have been, in the judgment of Rome herself, a doctrinal decision in the strict sense of the words. It is quite true that the Inquisition said that Galileo had done wrong in treating Copernicanism as a probable opinion, since by no means could an opinion be probable that had been declared and defined to be contrary to Holy Scripture; they also said in allusion to the decree of the Index that the books treating of the doctrine had been prohibited, and the doctrine—*i.e.* Copernicanism—had been declared false and altogether contrary to sacred and Divine Scripture. But a stream cannot rise higher than its source; and the Inquisition itself, having no other powers but those entrusted to it by the Pope, had no authority to put any more stringent interpretation on the decree of 1616 than what it already bore. So far as its actual wording goes, it is palpably a disciplinary decree, though founded on a doctrinal reason; and when the Inquisition cited it as if it were more than this, their language must be interpreted in accordance with the facts of the case; that is, as meaning that for the *purposes of discipline*, and for all practical intents and purposes, it had been defined that such a theory as that of Copernicus was inadmissible, and on the ground that it was contrary to Scripture as hitherto understood. But a decision of that nature is not irrevocable; it holds good as long as the ecclesiastical authorities determine it should do so, and no longer.

Rome must know her own mind, Mr. Roberts says; and she has shown her own mind, and borne out the construction I am putting on her acts, by further and subsequent action; for, after suspending the prohibitions against Copernicanism—or modifying them—in 1757, a distinct permission was given in 1820 to teach the theory of the Earth's movement; and again, in 1822, the permission was repeated in a more formal manner, and with the express sanction of the Pope, Leo XII.

Now we know that doctrinal decrees, once fully sanctioned and promulgated by the Holy See, are irreversible; but disciplinary enactments are changed according to the needs of the time and the circumstances of the Christian world.* If, then, these decrees against the Copernican theory of astronomy have been practically repealed by a decision no less formal than that which called them originally into existence, it is certain that Rome, who knows her own mind as well after the lapse of two hundred years as after that of seventeen years, considered them as appertaining to the province of discipline and not to that of dogma.

Moreover, Pius IX., when addressing the Archbishop of Munich, must have been well aware of the above-named facts, and when he enunciated the simple rule that good Catholics ought to submit in conscience to the doctrinal decrees of the Roman Congregations—indeed, how can any one imagine the *rule* to be anything else?—he must in common sense be understood to be speaking of decrees wholly different in scope and character from those relating to the case of Galileo and the system of Copernicus.

It must, nevertheless, be observed that an argument has been adduced by Mr. Roberts, and repeated even by so eminent a writer as Mr. Mivart, as if it were something that threw a new and important light on the subject. It is that Pope Alexander

---

* I must not be understood as implying that even doctrinal decisions promulgated by the Roman Congregations *in their own name* are considered by theologians to be infallible; such character belonging only to decisions addressed by the Pope himself to the Church.

VII., on the 5th March, 1664, published a Bull—known as the Bull "Speculatores"—approving a new and authentic edition of the Index of prohibited books, which Index contained the decree of 1616, and also the monitum of 1620, ordering certain corrections in the work of Copernicus, so that the theory he advocated should be stated merely as a hypothesis — in the preamble of which monitum, however, it is stated that the principles of Copernicus, relating to the movement of the Earth, were contrary to the true and Catholic interpretation of Holy Scripture—and contained also an edict, signed by Bellarmine, prohibiting and condemning Kepler's work, "Epitome Astronomiæ Copernicanæ;" an edict of August, 1634, prohibiting Galileo's Dialogue; and in fine, a prohibition of all books teaching the movement of the Earth and the immobility of the Sun.

In the year following this Bull another Index was also published, in which the following words occur, under the head Libri, as being forbidden to the faithful: "Libri omnes, et quicumque libelli, commentarii, compositiones, consulta, epistolæ, glossæ, opuscula, orationes, responsa, tractatus, tam typis editi, quam manuscripti, continentes et tractantes infrascriptas materias, seu de infrascriptis materiis . . . De mobilitate terræ, et immobilitate Solis." This, of course, is very sweeping, as it includes all pamphlets and letters, and even writings in manuscript, advocating Copernicanism.

Now, in reply to all this, I think I may remark that even lay theologians know, or ought to know, that Papal Bulls are divided into two distinct classes—dogmatic and disciplinary. The first, according to the doctrine of the Catholic Church, are held to be infallible, but still only as regards the decisions on faith or morals therein laid down, and not in respect of the reasons alleged; the second stand in a totally different position, and are not considered, as a general rule, to be in any way infallible—in fact, they are liable at any time to be modified or recalled, as in the instance before us has actually happened. The Bull "Speculatores" is plainly a disciplinary one. But I may perhaps be allowed to quote one who is professedly a theologian—the Reverend Jeremiah Murphy, an Irish ecclesiastic of learning and ability—who, replying to Mr. Mivart in *The Nineteenth Century* of May, 1886, explains, at some length, the real nature of this Bull. He says: "This Bull, so far from being a special approbation of each decree contained in the Index to which it is prefixed, is not a special approbation of even one of them... It is a re-issue, by public authority, of all these decrees (those of the Index), but it leaves each decree just as it was... The Pope, after referring to the origin of the Index, says that at that time there was no catalogue, issued by public authority, embracing the prohibited books and condemned authors, on which account great confusion has arisen. Accordingly, with the advice of the Cardinals, the Pope, as he states, has decreed to issue a new

Index. This was done in order that people should 'have a clear knowledge of all that was done from the beginning in this matter,' also to facilitate references for readers and especially for booksellers. The Pope goes on to say that he confirmed and approved this same general Index as aforesaid, composed and revised by our order, and printed at our apostolic press.'"

Mr. Murphy adds: "No new decree is issued, no new obligation imposed, no change in the character of any of the decrees is made by this Bull.... No Catholic theologian would for a moment regard this Bull as equivalent to an approbation, by special mandate, of any decree contained in the volume to which it is prefixed.... The Bull is a purely disciplinary act, perfectly valid until it is cancelled by an authority equal to that which issued it, but it condemns no new error, and defines no new truth."

It may no doubt be urged that there have been certain indiscreet controversialists who have maintained that the Popes had nothing to do with the condemnation of Galileo or of the Copernican theory —that, in fact, it was all the work of the Cardinals.

The Bull "Speculatores" is a good *argumentum ad hominem* addressed to such persons, but no one who knows the facts of the case can take up or ought to take up such a position. As a matter of discipline, the Popes did give their sanction to the condemnation in question. The Congregations of the Index and of the Inquisition have no authority at all except so far as the Pope confers it on them; and whether he gives them the authority beforehand, or confirms their acts by subsequent approval, the principle is essentially the same. He delegates to them certain disciplinary powers, but he does not delegate, and has not the power to delegate, his prerogative of defining dogma, and enforcing its belief on the whole Catholic world.

I should not have dwelt at so much length on this particular point had it not been urged, with what I fear I must call much perverted ingenuity, by Mr. Roberts that the Copernican theory was condemned *ex cathedrâ*, as if it were a heresy, by the Pope himself; nor, again, is it willingly that I quote so frequently the same author's arguments with a view to their refutation. He has, however, stated the anti-Roman case with ability, and without descending to vulgar claptrap. If, then, his arguments are satisfactorily answered, there is no need of combating other antagonists.

But I do not at all shrink from considering another and most important question. I have shown clearly and conclusively that the decrees against Copernicanism were not definitions of faith; but I am bound to state now what I believe to have been the effect of them in their own undoubted sphere, that of ecclesiastical discipline. And here there are two distinct questions to deal with, which are perhaps sometimes mixed up together, but which ought to be kept separate.

One is this: What should have been the conduct of contemporary Catholics, supposed to be scientific men, during the period that the decrees were in force? The other: What opinion ought *we* now to form upon the whole transaction, viewing it retrospectively?

To begin with the first of these two. I have little doubt as to what ought to have been the conduct of such Catholics—viz., implicit obedience to the disciplinary rules of the Church so long as the superior authorities thought fit to enforce them. Thus no good Catholic could have read the forbidden books, whether by Galileo or by any other author, without obtaining the requisite permission — a permission which in these days, at any rate, is given with great readiness to well-educated persons. Still less could a conscientious Catholic publish a work advocating the Copernican theory as the true one, or as most probably the true one. What I think he might have done is to publish a treatise stating any purely astronomical or mathematical arguments which seemed to favour Copernicanism as a hypothesis, and, at the same time, professing his entire submission to the ecclesiastical authorities, and explicitly disclaiming any attempt to meddle with the interpretation of Scripture. A protest of some such nature as this was inserted in an edition of the "Principia" which was allowed to be published by two Fathers of the order of Minims, Le Seur and Jacquier, in the year 1742, when the decrees were still in force.

But the first step, and that the most fitting and

becoming, would have been to submit privately to the Roman authorities all the scientific arguments which the Catholic astronomer—supposing such to be the case—had discovered as throwing fresh light on the question. No one has a right to infer from the instance of Galileo, whose arguments were not all of them sound or convincing, that such an astronomer as I have imagined would have been treated with contempt or neglect, especially if he made it evident that he was wholly submissive to the decrees of the Index, or other Roman Congregations.

Some writers, and notably the late Dr. Ward, have maintained that besides outward submission, a certain "interior assent" was due to the decision of the Congregation of the Index — such assent, however, being different in kind from that given to an article of Faith.

I submit, however, that although the fact of a book being placed on the forbidden list requires from all good Catholics a respectful assent to the *principle* that the Church has a right to enact these rules of discipline, it does not require an interior act of intellectual approval. It is said that Bellarmine's great controversial work was for a short time placed on the Index on account of some unpalatable opinion expressed in it. Did he think it necessary to make an interior act of assent to the decree?

It is true that in the case of the works of Copernicus and others, the grounds for prohibiting them were stated; but I would ask, are we obliged to assent interiorly to the grounds alleged for such acts?

In saying this, I do not wish to contradict the opinion of those theologians who hold that the non-scientific Catholics of Galileo's age were bound, by what is termed "the piety of Faith," to give a certain interior assent to the pronouncements of the Roman Congregations; and that on the ground that such persons had no better evidence to act upon. Their assent then would be very much like that given by dutiful sons, not yet of age, to the opinions of their father; similar in kind though stronger in degree.

I am of course assuming the contemporary Catholics, whose case I am considering, to be men of an obedient and dutiful disposition.

I have confined myself so far to the decrees of the Index. The sentence of the Inquisition on Galileo affected himself alone. It was no doubt held up as an example *in terrorem* for the benefit of others; but strictly and immediately it concerned Galileo alone, and when he died, it died with him.

I now pass to the all-important question, what ought we to think of the whole proceeding, with all the light that has been thrown on it by the two centuries and a half that have since elapsed? Here, then, I have to steer a middle course between what I hold to be extreme opinions on opposite sides, each held by men of note, and men whose principles and character demand that they should be heard with respect. One opinion is that of the late Dr. Ward, whom I take as a representative man on his side, though he is not the only writer who has taken the view to which I allude, and it is to the effect that the Roman Congregations acted not only fully within their rights, not only within their legitimate sphere, but that, considering all the circumstances of their time, they acted wisely and prudently; that the fault was on the side of Galileo and his followers, and the Cardinals could not have done otherwise than they did.

The other and opposite opinion has been stated by no Catholic writer with greater force than by Mr. Mivart; and it amounts, so far as I understand it, to this: that the Church has no authority to interfere in matters relating to physical science, and that the issue of the Galileo case has proved the fallacy of her attempting to do so; that without entering into the discussion of what ought or what ought not to have been done in former times, we of the present generation have evidence sufficient to show us that scientific investigations should by right be free from the control of ecclesiastical authority. The distinguished author to whom I allude has somewhat modified his original statements, and so I am in some danger of misrepresenting him, but I think the above is a fair epitome of his views on the subject; and at any rate I feel myself justified in dealing with him as he appeared in the widely circulated periodical in which he first enunciated his opinions, excepting so far as he may have explicitly retracted what he then said (which I do not believe to be the fact).

I regret that it is my lot to differ from both these able writers. As against Mr. Mivart, I venture to maintain that the Church has a full right to control the study of physical science; as against the late Dr. Ward, that we are not called upon to defend the action of the Congregation of the Index or of the Inquisition in this particular instance.

I take Mr. Mivart first, and I may be permitted to say that had it not been for his somewhat aggressive article, I should not have ventured to publish my own views on the subject. I call it aggressive because, though the writer would doubtless disclaim such intention, it seemed as though he were determined, so to speak, to drive the ecclesiastical authorities into a corner, and leave them no honourable mode of exit; letting his readers infer that, because certain untenable decisions were once promulgated, it results that no further respect need now be paid to the same authorities when touching on similar questions. Now, it need scarcely be pointed out that no one would presume to treat the decision of secular courts—assuredly fallible as they are—in so contemptuous a way; and if any one practically did so, the executive of the country where it occurred, unless it had fallen into a condition of hopeless impotence, would speedily vindicate the rights of the courts so impugned. But if it should be urged that the two cases are not parallel, I prefer to confine my argument to ecclesiastical tribunals only. I maintain, then, that — always assuming the truth of the Catholic standpoint, which, with Mr. Mivart, I am justified in doing—the Church has an obvious right to interfere with and to regulate the study of physical science and the promulgation of scientific theories. It would be more consistent and more intelligible to deny the right of the Church to proscribe any theories whatever, or to forbid the reading of any books, however profane, than to admit it in all other matters, but deny it in the one case of physical science.

I yield to no one in feeling a deep interest in science generally, and especially astronomy, the Queen of Sciences, as it is sometimes called; many sciences, and astronomy in particular, well deserve to be studied for their own sake, and for the intellectual profit and pleasure they convey to the mind, putting aside all questions of practical utility. And yet if we are to measure all the advantages derivable from the study of natural science against the mighty and momentous issues which Religion brings before us, it seems to me that in so doing we are measuring some finite quantity with that which transcends all our powers of comparison because it is not only vast but simply *infinite.* If you do not believe Religion, or at least revealed Religion, to be true, then I understand your worshipping science, or like the Positivists worshipping Humanity, or any idol you choose to con-

statute; but I do not understand a Christian's doing so, that is, a Christian in the strict and legitimate sense of the word. Pursue science by all means, as you pursue literature, art, or any other innocent human study, but do not make it such an idol as to obscure your perception of spiritual truths.

And to take the Copernican theory in particular: profoundly interesting as it is, let us ask ourselves not merely whether it is so important as to require that all religious considerations should give way before it, but whether the knowledge of its truth, which we now possess, adds very materially to the sum total of human happiness. Let us then, for a moment, think how many men among the millions that people this Earth, or if we please to limit our inquiry, how many among the civilised nations of the Earth understand anything whatever about the motions of the heavenly bodies. No doubt, in England, and probably many other countries, the elementary books that are taught to children state in a rough general way that the Earth, like other planets, goes round the Sun in the space of one year, and revolves on its axis in twenty-four hours. So far, so good. Suppose you asked those, who as children have learned these facts, a few ordinary questions in astronomy—I do not mean things relating to celestial distances, or anything that can be learnt by heart, but questions requiring thought—how many would be able to answer you? How many, for example, could explain such a familiar phenomenon as the harvest moon?—though that has nothing to do with the Copernican theory. How many could explain the precession of the equinoxes? Suppose yourself in a room full of educated persons, but not specially instructed in science, how many could state correctly the first law of motion?*

It is unnecessary to multiply instances; astronomy is obviously a science adapted not to the multitude of mankind, but to the comparatively few, who reflect and think. If, then, some check were given in the seventeenth century, by the action of the ecclesiastical authorities in Rome, to the progress of physical astronomy, we must surely allow that the injury to human welfare and human happiness was so small that we need not dwell upon it.

Mr. Mivart tells us that Descartes was deterred for some time from publishing his work. Now Descartes, as a pure mathematician, stands in the highest rank. The method which he invented of applying algebraical

---

* A curious instance of popular unacquaintance with astronomy was afforded some months ago, when the planet Venus, which one would think was a well-known object to most people, was mistaken for "the Star of Bethlehem;" and this mistake was by no means confined to the ignorant, but was shared by persons of education.

The planet was at the time a brilliant "morning star;" and the effect on the eye is more striking in these circumstances than when it is seen, as is very commonly the case, in the evening, shortly after sunset. I suppose this would account in some measure for the delusion.

In clearer and finer skies than those of England, Venus is sometimes so brilliant in the early morning as to startle an unaccustomed observer.

analysis to geometry has facilitated calculation to an extent impossible to over-estimate; notwithstanding the discovery and adoption of other and rival methods, that of Descartes still holds its own, and will probably do so as long as the science of mathematics is cultivated.

But as an astronomer, Descartes can be allowed no such pre-eminence; his work on Vortices was actually a retrograde step, and in France it even hindered for a considerable time the reception of the true doctrine of universal gravitation. So that we may well say if Descartes had never published his book at all, physical astronomy would have been the gainer rather than the loser.

Mr. Mivart writes as if he were under some apprehension that the Church would interfere with his favourite study of biology. I believe his fears are unfounded. The Roman ecclesiastical authorities are doubtless conscious of the fact that there is a great moral chasm between the Europe of the seventeenth century and the Europe of this day. The means that were adapted for contending against error, real or supposed, two hundred and fifty years ago, are inapplicable in the present age. Experience has shown that false scientific theories are pretty sure to be demolished, time enough being allowed, either by the internal dissensions of their own supporters, or by the sharp criticism of the supporters of some antagonistic theory; or, perhaps, the triumphant progress of new discoveries. Works of a particularly offensive or irreligious character may from time to time be put on the Index of prohibited books; but the Church will probably leave purely scientific hypotheses of all kinds to find their own level, and to stand or fall, as the case may be.

There remains one objection, brought forward by Mr. Roberts, which I may notice. It is one of the condemned propositions recited in the well-known "Syllabus," that the decrees of the Apostolic See and the Roman Congregations hinder the free progress of science. But can any one honestly say that they do? It is one thing to admit that the Church may for certain reasons put an occasional and temporary check on the study of some particular science; another, to accuse her of generally and systematically hindering the progress of knowledge; for be it observed that the Latin word, *scientia*, from which the above is translated, does not merely mean physical science.

The Catholic Church has put strong restrictions on the use of vernacular translations of Holy Scripture—restrictions which, though greatly modified in practice, are not yet abolished — but a proposition stating broadly that the Church was opposed to the study of Scripture would be condemned, and very justly so.

I now come to deal with the other extreme opinion, if I may venture so to call it—that maintained by the late Dr. Ward, and others—to the effect that not only has the Church a right to condemn this or that scientific theory, but that the exercise of such right, as practically exemplified in the prohibition of certain

Copernican works, and in the condemnation of Galileo, was sound and prudent, and what might reasonably have been expected. I am not sure whether Dr. Ward goes quite so far as regards the condemnation of Galileo by the Inquisition; but he does so in respect of the previous decree of 1616. His ground is that at that period the Copernican doctrine was, even scientifically speaking, improbable; while it gave a shock to those who venerated the traditional interpretation of Holy Scripture. Few men have a greater respect than myself for the memory of the able writer whose views I am about to criticise; but physical science was not his strong point. His knowledge of metaphysical philosophy was great; so, too, was his knowledge of dogmatic theology; but he does not appear to have been well versed in natural science, and with that modesty which is a characteristic of sound and solid learning, he was careful never to pretend acquaintance with any particular branch of knowledge, unless he really possessed it.

He was at times even scrupulous in expressing his acknowledgments for the assistance he had received from others in matters outside the limits of his own studies; as also in admitting an error if he felt really guilty of one; showing therein a candour and honesty of purpose that we do not always meet with. So much I say in tribute to an honoured memory. I now proceed to state why I cannot follow his views. It is surely paradoxical, to say the least of it, to maintain that an opinion is theologically false but scientifically true; or to state the case more accurately, to maintain that it was right to condemn as contrary to Scripture what has since turned out to be true—assuming, of course, this latter to be the fact, which Dr. Ward fully admitted. It may doubtless be pleaded in mitigation that the Cardinals only meant that the opinion was contrary to the *traditional* interpretation of Scripture, and that it was just conceivable that the method of interpretation would have to be revised hereafter; and we have seen that Bellarmine's letter to Foscarini points decidedly in that direction. Nevertheless, the decree on the face of it appears to imply more than this, and when coupled with the subsequent condemnation of Galileo, and strengthened by the repeated prohibition, even in more stringent terms, of all works favouring the Copernican theory, it obviously dealt as heavy a blow at the doctrine of the Earth's diurnal and annual movement, as could well have been done, short of a dogmatic decision. It may be quite true that if Galileo had been more prudent and judicious, much of this would have been averted, and possibly the decree of 1616 might have been modified or suspended a century earlier than it actually was so. But without discussing imaginary possibilities, we take the facts as they stand.

Now to give one or two specimens of Dr. Ward's mode of writing on this subject. He says (after stating correctly the Catholic principle that books theologically unsound should be kept from persons who are not specially qualified to read them without injury): " In Galileo's time all books which advocated the truth of Copernicanism were theologically unsound. And a most important service was done by preserving the Catholic flock free from the plague; free from a most false, proud, irreverent, and dangerous principle of Scriptural interpretation."— *Dublin Review*, October, 1865.

I have already said that Galileo would have been wiser if he had entirely left alone the question of the interpretation of Scripture; but it must always be remembered that it was not he but his opponents who commenced the discussion on that particular head. They were weak in the astronomical argument; and they tried to damage their opponent by attacking him on Scriptural grounds. It is difficult to understand what Dr. Ward means by the forcible language I have just quoted, nor how a principle of Scriptural interpretation, adopted at the present day by every one, could have been in Galileo's time false, proud, irreverent, and dangerous.* Dr. Ward grounds

* Dr. Ward makes a curious mistake in one point; he speaks in one of the articles of *The Dublin Review* (which he then edited) of Copernicanism as destroying the old ideas as to *above and below;* that is to say, for instance, your idea of ascending on high towards heaven was thereby nullified, and ascending from the surface of the earth meant going in any direction which the earth's rotation might place above your head at any particular moment. But Dr. Ward, who was doubtless thinking of the very old and exploded notion that the earth was a flat surface, does not seem to have been aware that this objection applies in principle to the Ptolemaic

his argument, however, on an idea that he had, to the effect that the Copernican system in Galileo's day was "scientifically unlikely:" this, however, is just the reverse of the truth. It was *unproved;* and, as I have repeatedly said, it is not even now proved to absolute demonstration.

It is also true that certain most powerful arguments for it were not then available, as I shall hereafter have occasion to show at more length; but it was not scientifically unlikely. Galileo had indirectly damaged the cause by using a certain erroneous argument in its favour; but then his discoveries had simply pulverised the great rival system of Ptolemy, and no astronomer, who knew what he was about, could do otherwise than choose between Copernicus and Tycho Brahé, each of these being of course somewhat modified in detail. Now the theory of Tycho Brahé was a new one, still newer than that of Copernicus, and had all the appearance of a temporary makeshift; it was not probable that it would receive much approbation in the long run, as in fact it never did. Probability (I mean, of course, in a purely scientific sense) pointed strongly

---

system also; Ptolemy knew that the earth was spherical in its shape, and consequently that what would be *above* a person in the eastern parts of India, to take an example, would be widely different from that which would be so at the westernmost point of Africa. It may, however, be admitted that an additional cause for bewilderment was presented by the diurnal rotation of the Earth, since it then appeared that the same point in space *above* you at noon would be far away *below* you at midnight.

to the Copernican theory even in Galileo's time; and after Kepler's celebrated laws had been published, far more strongly still than before. Of course, as Dr. Ward points out, there *may* be other reasons of so cogent a nature as to outweigh *scientific* probability; but that is not now the question: he denies even the existence of this latter at the period we are treating of; and on this point he was evidently misinformed.

It is said that the Cardinals of the Index or Inquisition consulted some astronomers before formulating their decrees, and this is likely enough; as there is *odium medicum* in these days, there was doubtless *odium astronomicum* in those days.

And we may easily imagine how the philosophers who believed in the infallibility of Aristotle looked with horror and perhaps contempt on the School of Galileo. If people once persuade themselves that physical science is to be learnt merely from tradition, or from *à priori* arguments, they will naturally have an antipathy to the discoveries made by actual observation and experiment. If men such as these were called in to advise the Cardinals, we may well admit it as a mitigating circumstance, forbidding us to pass a severe judgment on the conduct of the ecclesiastical tribunals. It is no part of my contention, and indeed the very reverse, to lay excessive blame on the Congregations of the Index and Inquisition; but neither, on the other hand, do I understand why we should give them our unqualified approval.

I feel that the opinion I have expressed above, and which might otherwise be considered by some persons as presumptuous towards the ecclesiastical authorities, receives great confirmation, and at the same time what is tantamount to an acquittal from all disrespect to the Church and her authority, by the following extract which I give from the article entitled, "Dr. Mivart on Faith and Science," published in the October number of *The Dublin Review* (1887), by the Bishop of Newport and Menevia, the Right Rev. J. C. Hedley. Not only does the high character of the author, both as a theologian and a man of scientific knowledge, give a sanction to all that is contained in the article, but the Review in which it appears, having for its proprietor another Bishop and an able ecclesiastic for its acting editor, carries with it a stamp of Catholic authority such as few periodicals possess. After some other remarks the Bishop of Newport proceeds thus:

> I do not by any means wish to deny that the case of Galileo has had an important effect on the action of Church authorities. It seems quite clear that it has made them more cautious in pronouncing on the interpretation of Scripture when the sacred text speaks of natural phenomena. The reason of this is not so much the fact that science has proved authority wrong in one case, as because that case, taking it with all its circumstances, was one the like of which can never happen again. The Galilean controversy marked the close of a period and the opening of a new one. The heliocentric view was the first step in modern scientific expression. Before the days of Galileo men spoke of what they saw with the naked eye, and on the surface of things; thenceforth they were to use the telescope and the microscope; they investigated the bowels of the earth and the distances of the

heavens. It was a far-reaching and most pregnant generalisation when men first took in the idea that the arrangements which their books had hitherto called by the expression "nature" were merely a very few of the most obvious aspects of a vast organisation, which could be, and which must be, searched into by observation. At once a multitude of familiar phrases lost their meaning, and many accepted truths had to be dethroned.

And the effect of the discussion in the days of Galileo was not only to make men revise their formularies about the earth's motion, but to impress them most forcibly with the possibility that such a process might have to be gone through about a very large number of other things. The prevailing views were held by the Church authorities as by every one else. They were not really a part of the Divine revelation. Some people thought they were, and (we may admit it was a misfortune) the very authorities who had to pronounce, used language which was to some extent mistaken in the same direction. On the other hand, it is clear now that men of mark and standing asserted over and over again, that the new theories need not in any point contradict Holy Scripture. It was a matter which was not clear all at once. It is often not immediately evident that novel scientific views do or do not contradict Revelation. They have to be made precise, to be qualified, to be analysed, and that by fallible men. During the process many Catholics will naturally make mistakes, and there is no reason why, now and then, Church authority itself should not make a mistake in this particular matter. When the requisite reflection has had time to be made, then it is seen, as it was in the case of the views under discussion, that what was held by Catholic persons was something quite apart from Catholic faith. And we have no objection to admit that reflection was quickened, and caution was deepened by the case of Galileo. In this sense, and not in any other, that case may be called "emancipatory." If the Church authorities ever feel themselves called upon to pronounce on the dates or the authorship of the Hexateuch, or on the formation of Adam's body, they will proceed—we may say it without suspicion of undutifulness—with more enlightened minds than the Congregations which condemned Galileo.

The teaching Church is composed of fallible men, who must sometimes, in certain departments, make mistakes, and who must learn by experience as other men learn. The part of a dutiful

Catholic is to lessen the effect of mistaken decisions by prudent silence or respectful remonstrance in the proper quarter, and not to make scandal worse by inept generalisations and unnecessary bitterness.

Further on, the Bishop says:

I do not decline to face the difficulty of Galileo's compulsory retractation. It seems to me that either Galileo had sufficiently strong reasons to prevent his mind from making the retractation or not. I think it possible he had not. It does not seem that he had anything like evidence that the earth moved. If he had not, there was no reason why he should not assent to a strong expression of authority, that authority being one to which he owed filial obedience. . . . Still, if Galileo had present to his mind strong proof of the correctness of his own teachings, I do not hesitate to say that he was wrong, and, indeed, committed sin, in making the retractation demanded.

On the purely astronomical question whether Galileo had evidence that the Earth moved, I presume that the Bishop means *conclusive* evidence; for evidence of some kind he surely had; not conclusive, it is true, but good as far as it went. Long before Galileo was tried by the tribunal of the Inquisition, his contemporary, Kepler, had published those important astronomical laws which still bear his name, and which tended powerfully to corroborate the theory of the Earth's motion. Apart, however, from this, as I have already intimated, I think there was good ground for the opinion in question.

This, however, is to some extent a digression. I have quoted the Bishop principally in order to strengthen, by his high authority, the line of argument I have ventured to pursue, which, in effect, is this: that the principle on which the Roman Congregations acted in Galileo's case was sound, but the application of it in the particular instance mistaken and injudicious.

I may also be permitted to cite, as confirming my own opinion, the words of the distinguished writer to whom, in common with all students of the Galileo case, I am so much indebted, M. Henri de l'Épinois. They do not, of course, possess the same theological authority as that of the prelate I have just quoted, but, coming from a learned Catholic layman, they are well worthy of attention. These are his words:

> Galilée, en établissant les principes de mécanique qui sont ses titres de gloire, comme en soutenant la doctrine de Copernic, a rencontré pour adversaires déclarés les partisans de la philosophie d'Aristote, qui combattaient aussi bien Képler à Tubingue, et Descartes en Hollande. Ils appelèrent à leur aide des textes de l'Écriture, les opposèrent aux affirmations de Galilée. Pour se défendre celui-ci voulut expliquer ces textes. Dès lors, il changeait l'interprétation jusque-là admise par l'Église et éveillait les justes susceptibilités des Catholiques. Avait-il raison? Avait-il tort? Il avait tort dans plusieurs de ses propositions, et sa conduite manqua souvent de prudence; il avait évidemment raison dans sa doctrine fondamentale. En fait le tribunal s'est trompé en condamnant comme fausse et contraire à l'Écriture une doctrine vraie et qui pouvait s'accorder avec les textes sacrés. Il a manqué de prudence en se montrant trop circonspect, et a ainsi dépassé le but. Il faut toutefois le remarquer. Aujourd'hui il est facile de dire: le tribunal a eu tort; mais en 1616, en 1633, la plupart des savants, les Universités et les Académies disaient: il a raison. . . .
>
> Tous les témoignages contemporains nous montrent que deux pensées, deux opinions, deux influences étaient en présence: d'un côté les Aristotéliciens acharnés contre Galilée, détestant ses principes, voulant les anéantir; de l'autre les papes, les cardinaux,

pleins d'estime pour Galilée, mais qui voulaient prévenir les fâcheuses conséquences de sa doctrine.

Selon que l'une ou l'autre de ces influences domina dans les conseils, on tint une conduite différente : tantôt sévère et rigoureuse, tantôt douce et indulgente. Mais il n'y eut point là, comme on le prétend encore, de lutte entre la science et le Catholicisme ; la question fut débattue entre la science et l'Aristotélisme.*

It was not till the year 1757 that any authoritative step was taken to relax the prohibitions imposed by the Index on the works advocating the Copernican system. This was more than a century after the condemnation of Galileo, seventy years after the publication of the "Principia," and thirty years after the discovery of the aberration of light. Even Dr. Ward allows that it might have been more prudent to remove the prohibitions some forty or fifty years sooner than was actually the case. No one, he observes, supposes the Church to be infallible in mere matters of *prudence*, and I think that in making this statement, which, I presume, every theologian would at once endorse, he half admits the principle for which I contend ; for if the Roman authorities could err in point of prudence in leaving the censure so long in force, might they not err— I mean, of course, as to the prudent administration of discipline—in inflicting those censures at all, or at any rate in applying them so rigorously in practice as was done in the instance of Galileo ?

* Quoted from an article in the "Revue des Questions Historiques," 1867, " Galilée, son Procès, sa Condemnation, d'après des documents inédits," by M. Henri de l'Épinois.

However, be this as it may, in the year 1757 the relaxation of the censures took place; in 1820, on the 16th August, a distinct permission was given for teaching the movement of the Earth; and again on the 17th September, 1822, a re-examination of the whole subject having taken place, a decree appeared, sanctioned by the Pope, Leo XII., in which the Inquisitors General, in conformity with the decrees of 1757 and 1820, declared that the printing and publishing at Rome of works treating of the movement of the Earth and the immobility of the Sun, according to the opinion of modern astronomers, was henceforth permitted. Thus the decree of 1616 was practically abrogated.

Mr. Mivart, among other remarks on the proceedings in Galileo's case, says that no amends were ever made by the authorities of the Church for the injustice done to the philosopher, but he does not state what kind of amends or what sort of apology he expected. If he means that no personal reparation was made to Galileo, that is doubtless true; nor was any sacrifice ever offered to his Manes. Indeed, it must be allowed that the ecclesiastical authorities hindered the erection, after his decease, of a monument in his honour. Nor is this a matter for surprise; it may be taken for granted that the object of those who desired to erect the monument was to pay an especial tribute of respect to the deceased astronomer as one who had suffered unjustly; and that was precisely what the Pope and Cardinals of that age would not for a moment admit.

No personal amends, then, were made to Galileo in life or in death; but I think this was not the point to which Mr. Mivart intended to allude. I believe he had in his mind a different sort of reparation—that, namely, supposed to be owing to the injured cause of Science. If that be so, then I can only say that he must have been unaware of the facts above mentioned, of the proceedings taken in Rome in 1757, in 1820, and in 1822.

The adjustment of the relations of revealed Religion with physical Science is often perplexing, owing partly to mistaken zeal in insisting on particular interpretations of certain passages in Holy Scripture, and partly to the prevalence, at different times, of doubtful scientific theories, which flourish for a time, and then fade away because they fail to stand the test of continued and rigorous investigation.

Instances of both these will readily occur to the mind, and the Copernican theory in the seventeenth century will be a prominent one, as coming under the first of the two heads. But it is not fair, as I have already argued, to be too severe upon the men who clung with tenacity to the old traditional interpretation of Scripture. It is, in fact, only right so to cling until some just reason is shown for introducing a fresh interpretation. In this case there were some good reasons, no doubt; but there were also bad reasons alleged, and, as we have seen, Galileo, with all his great ability and mechanical knowledge so far beyond his age, could yet damage his cause with unsound arguments.

Such being the case, amidst the whirlpool of good and bad arguments—that drawn from the tides being by no means the only one of the latter class—it is not astonishing that even able and intelligent men were misled.

The antipathy to adopting a new system of the universe—a system which demolished many cherished ideas and traditional opinions—was overwhelmingly strong; the reasons uncertain, or, at least, inconclusive. The discoveries of Galileo had, no doubt, overthrown the system of Ptolemy, but they had not established that of Copernicus, so long as there remained what may be called the tentative theory of Tycho Brahé, who was one of the greatest observers of his day. Though he did not unravel the true cause of the motions of the heavenly bodies, and went, in fact, in a wrong direction, we must never forget the important services he rendered to science. He was the first to employ refraction as a correction to the apparent positions of the celestial bodies; his collection of instruments, on which he had expended the whole of his private fortune, was the finest that had ever yet been seen; and, in fact, his observations, utilised by others, had a great share in leading to the discovery of the real nature of the planetary movements.* Small blame, then, must be meted out to those who held on for a time to the system excogitated by so enlightened a man. I do not mean to deny what I have already stated—that the Cardinals who put on the Index of forbidden books the works of Copernicus and others, and those who condemned Galileo, were unable, astronomically speaking, to read the signs of the times. All I am asserting is that there was much, even from a scientific point of view, to excuse their inability.

They put forward as their main objection that the new theory contradicted Holy Scripture, and adhered to that rigidly literal interpretation of it, which has since then been necessarily given up, and which seems somewhat strange to us, accustomed as we now are to a far greater latitude of interpretation than they even dreamed of. We who have learned that the six days of Creation are not to be taken in their strict sense;† who have sound reason for holding that the Deluge was only universal in the sense of covering that part of the earth then inhabited by the

---

* Tycho Brahé discovered two out of the principal inequalities in the Moon's motion—known to astronomers as the Variation and the Annual Equation; the third, which is the most obvious of all and is called the Evection, was discovered by Ptolemy.

† The figurative interpretation, however, in this instance is as old as St. Augustine, though his speculations lead him to a different conclusion from that of modern scientific men; namely, that of supposing the actual creation to be the work of one moment.

human race; and who are told by some people, including learned ecclesiastics, that it was more restricted in its operation even than this; and who finally hear it said by men of undoubted orthodoxy that the evolution of man from some lower animal, so far as his *body* is concerned and so long as you do not include his soul and his rational faculties, is consistent with the Christian faith—we, I say, who are familiar with these non-literal interpretations of Scripture, find it difficult to comprehend the standpoint adopted and maintained with such tenacity by the Cardinals of the seventeenth century.

There were, moreover, other very cogent reasons which, though not put prominently forward, may well have worked upon their minds; reasons, indeed, which must strike the really thoughtful man. Let us consider this one point. In old times, when the Earth was believed to be the actual centre of the physical universe, it was easy to suppose that it was the sole abode of life. But if you believe that the Earth, far from being such a centre, is only one amongst many planets revolving round the Sun; and, further, that the Sun himself is only one of a mighty host of stars, some of which may have planets revolving round them, you naturally ask yourself immediately, are none of these worlds inhabited except our Earth? Truly Scripture says nothing to contradict the opinion that there are inhabitants and rational creatures to be found elsewhere; but, nevertheless, the history of the Creation and Redemption of the human race reads as if such creatures, intelligent beings like ourselves, lived upon this Earth, and nowhere besides.

I know not how far thoughts and speculations of this nature passed through the minds of the ecclesiastics, and other men of religious feeling, in the age of Galileo. They have since then been sifted more or less by scientific men, and various opinions have been suggested. Some went so far as to think it possible that the Sun was inhabited. So able an astronomer as Arago, to say nothing of others, thought such might be the fact. No one thinks so now. The tendency of modern thought, strictly speaking *modern* (that is, the most recent), is rather to discredit such imaginations. The various observations made upon the Sun, including those made by the use of the spectroscope, have shown that the supposition of his being inhabited is simply incredible. For other reasons the same result has been reached with regard to the Moon. Then as to the planets, although there are no such cogent reasons, we may fairly say that the probability is against any one of them being at the present moment fitted for the habitation of such a creature as man. Some persons would make an exception in favour of Mars, where a recent French observer imagines he has detected signs of work as if by human hands—a stretch indeed of imagination.

But the planets are probably not all in the same stage of what may be termed geological history. Some may very possibly be in the same state in which the Earth was a few millions of years ago, long before it was fitted for the reception of man on its surface, or, indeed, for that of any of the higher mammalia. The Earth had had a long history, and had undergone vast changes, ranging perhaps over many millions of years, before man appeared on the scene; and the period that has elapsed since that event, whatever the date of it may be, is simply nothing in comparison of the ages that had previously rolled by since the first moment when the darkness gave way, and the light appeared. It is, then, far from unlikely that our own Earth is the only planet in the solar system which at the present time is suitable for the habitation of man, or creatures resembling him.*

Passing then from our own system, we come to the myriads of suns, some, we may well believe, far greater than our Sun, which are spread through the realms of space.† Many of these we may reasonably suppose are surrounded by planets, and in one or two cases there are special reasons for thinking that some opaque body intervenes occasionally between the star and ourselves. But the conditions under which several of the stars (we know not how many) exist, is very different from that to which we are accustomed here with our own Sun. There are double stars which

* It is, I think, Mr. Proctor who uses this argument in one of his works, to prove how very doubtful a thing is the existence of highly organised and rational beings on the other planets.

† It is quite possible, as Mr. Lockyer has recently argued, that many objects that appear to us as stars, are in reality nebulæ in a more or less advanced stage of condensation.

appear to revolve round a common centre of gravity, a system of two suns. Have each of them, or have both of them in common, a set of planets moving round them? Who can tell? And where there are stars with planets accompanying them, does any one know in what state those planets are? The whole subject, however interesting as a speculation, is shrouded in impenetrable mystery.

From all this it follows that although there certainly may be rational and intellectual inhabitants on some or other of these distant worlds, yet, on the other hand, there *may not* be. And it is perfectly possible that our Earth, minute little object as it is, comparatively speaking, may still be the great and favoured life-house of the universe, the *moral*, though not *material*, centre. That the Earth is not the physical centre of the universe we now are well aware; nor is the Sun the centre; nor, indeed, do we know whether there is any such centre at all. There is good reason for thinking that the Sun, with his attendant planets, is in motion in a certain direction in space; and I may observe that this direction is not in the plane of the Earth's orbit, or anything near it; so that though the Earth describes an elliptical orbit with regard to the Sun, its path in space is some kind of spiral curve, that is as it would appear to a being poised for a time in some point of space far away outside our orbit, having the necessary powers of vision, and having a plane of reference from which he could take his observations.

What else this gifted being might see—whether he would observe some great central body round which the whole of the heavenly bodies revolve, or, as seems more probable, would detect, instead of one, many centres, each with its own group—all this we do not and cannot know, and we must be content, at least so long as our life here below continues, to remain in profound ignorance.

Seeing, then, how wide in extent and how difficult of solution are some of the speculative problems, originating in the Copernican theory, it can be no matter of surprise that the ecclesiastics of the seventeenth century recoiled from it with more than common aversion.

CHAPTER V.

As a sequel to the story of Galileo, I think it may be interesting to inquire what the evidence, as *we now have it*, proves with regard to the truth of the Copernican theory, there being two opposite and contradictory errors on this subject, and these not merely popular errors, but shared to some extent by educated and otherwise learned men. But I must, before proceeding, remind my readers that I use the word *Copernican* simply to signify the system of modern astronomy, that in which the Sun is the centre round which the Earth and the other planets revolve, and not as meaning the precise theory of Copernicus, which (as I have said) was overthrown by Kepler, when he discovered that the planetary orbits were not circular but elliptical, the Sun, moreover, not being strictly in the centre, but in one of the foci of the orbit.

Now it is a plain fact, which all persons must perceive, that either the Earth revolves on its axis in twenty-four hours (more accurately 23 hours 56 mins. 5 secs.), or else that the whole of the celestial bodies are carried round the Earth in that same time. It is also a fact no less perceptible to *careful* observers, that either the Sun goes round the Earth in the course of a year, or else that the Earth goes round the Sun. The question is how these facts are to be accounted for.

The first of the two errors I have just mentioned is that which supposes the Copernican theory to have been directly and conclusively proved. This I imagine to be very common, and to arise from the elementary books learnt by schoolboys, which state (naturally enough) the modern theory of astronomy without the reasons that support it.

We need not dwell long on this point. Persons who have got this erroneous impression misunderstand the nature of the evidence. Some things in astronomy can be positively proved from observation, as, for instance, the existence of sun-spots. Many things in mechanics, chemistry, optics, and other branches of physical study can be demonstrated by experiment. The motion of the Earth round the Sun cannot, however, be so treated. It is inferred, and very rightly so, from the fact that it explains completely and easily all the observed phenomena, while, on the other hand, there are certain things which, as *far as our present knowledge goes*, cannot be explained in any other way; and the same argument applies to the rotation of the Earth on its axis. But though all this is perfectly clear so far, who can possibly say that as science progresses some explanation may not be hereafter found consistent with the antagonistic theory—consistent, let us say, with the system of Tycho Brabé, or some modification of it?

I need not add that I consider the future discovery of such explanation as so improbable, that one may practically dismiss the idea, but I should be sorry to deny it as being conceivably possible.

The other, and opposite, error is that of certain well-meaning but ill-informed persons, who imagine that the Copernican theory is even now doubtful and liable to be overthrown—liable, I mean, in a real and practical sense, and not by distant contingencies, such as those at which I have just hinted, and which may be considered as shadowy and intangible. I do not suppose that amongst educated men there are many such scientific recusants; but at any rate it may be useful to give a short summary of the evidence on which the Copernican conclusion is based. In doing this I fear I shall tire the patience of my readers by partly repeating Galileo's own arguments, which I have already quoted in discussing the Dialogue. This cannot easily be avoided, for much of his reasoning is so sound and so forcible, that after the lapse of more than two centuries we can add but little to it. On the other hand, there are grave mistakes that must be shunned; and, moreover, there have been discoveries made since the day when the Dialogue was written, of inestimable importance.

The best way of treating the question is to resume the history of astronomical research from the point where we dropped it; that is, at the time when Galileo first made known to the world the result of his observations.

It ought to be clearly understood that from the moment the telescope was turned on the heavens, the old system of astronomy was doomed, and nothing could finally have saved it. For a time prejudice and other more creditable feelings kept it floating on the sea of speculation, but such a state of things could not last; and the startling information that men like Galileo, Fabricius, and Scheiner imparted to the scientific world, could not fail to expel the old theory of the universe from the minds of men— at least, men of intellectual capacity—gradually and slowly, but yet most surely.

Now we have seen what the revelations were which the telescope at once displayed, even in its comparatively rude and imperfect state. There were the spots on the Sun, the satellites of Jupiter, the phases of Venus, the greater apparent size of the superior planets (Mars and the rest) when on the opposite side of the Earth from the Sun, this last phenomenon being quite inconsistent with the system of Ptolemy.

One consequence of all this was that the less enlightened men of the old school indulged in a violent antipathy to the new-fangled instrument, which threatened to overthrow their time-honoured traditions, and simply refused to believe in the telescope and its results. Thus the principal professor of philosophy at Padua, when invited by Galileo to look through his glass at the Moon and the planets, pertinaciously refused to do so. Simplicio, who, of course, represents in the Dialogue the prejudices of men of this stamp, admits (as we have seen) his feelings on this subject, and his suspicions that the new discoveries were to be attributed to optical errors. He was willing to be corrected if mistaken, but such had hitherto been his opinion.

It was not, however, to be expected that men of sound sense would allow themselves to be misled for any length of time by fallacies such as these. Continued observations carefully made are sure to correct mere optical errors, and after a reasonable interval it must have been evident that the phenomena discerned through the telescope were facts that had to be dealt with—not phantoms to be ignored.

Thus, when it was found that the planet Venus presented to the eye phases such as the Moon does, instead of always appearing like a round body, it became evident that she revolved, not as Ptolemy supposed, round the Earth, but round the Sun, an inference subsequently confirmed by the observation of her transits over the Sun's disc.

This being so, the adherents of Ptolemy had to meet this difficulty: here was a planet much nearer to the Earth than to the Sun,* and yet revolving round the latter in preference to the former. There was clearly, then, *some* attractive force belonging to the Sun (whatever its nature might be), greater

---

* The *relative* distances could be computed geometrically, even before the absolute distances were known, and in fact were so; Kepler's third law affords a simple rule for calculating them, but they were known even previously.

than that of the Earth, which Venus obeyed; the same was true of Mercury, with the difference that this planet was much nearer to the Sun. Then as regards the superior planets, Mars, Jupiter, Saturn, the probability that the Sun was the great central power that controlled their movements was a very strong one. There is but little to add on these topics to Galileo's own forcible argument in the third day's dialogue; he is, however, inaccurate in his figures, and states that Mars appears sixty times as large when in opposition to the Sun, as at conjunction. More recent observations have shown that he appears rather more than thirty times as large when at his nearest point to the Earth, than he does when near his conjunction with the Sun, and consequently at his farthest point from the Earth; but this variation is quite sufficient for the argument, and proves incontestably that if Mars revolves round the Earth as in any way the centre of his orbit, it must be in an ellipse of so great eccentricity as no one could reasonably imagine him to do; indeed, the anti-Copernicans of Galileo's day knew nothing of the elliptic motions of the planets; neither, as we have seen, did Galileo himself.

The same argument, drawn from the apparent size of the planet at different periods, applies also to Jupiter and Saturn—the other exterior planets were discovered much later—only not so strikingly as in the case of Mars. The improbability, if we once admit that all the planets revolve round the

Sun, that the Earth, occupying the position it does, should be at rest, while the Sun, controlling the motions of the planets (vast bodies, some of them), circled, nevertheless, round the Earth; the improbability, I say, of this is so great as to be almost overwhelming; at any rate, unless the difficulties of the counter hypothesis were shown to be insurmountable, which, as we know, is far from being the case. It was of course possible, without going the lengths of the Paduan professor, and setting oneself against the telescope altogether, to admit the facts but deny the inferences; to grant, for instance, that Mars appeared to have a diameter more than six times as great in one position as in another, and to attribute it, as I hinted just now, to some extraordinary eccentricity in his orbit round the Earth; but it is not wise to look through a telescope with the eyes of the body open and the eyes of the mind closed; and generally it is but right to be guided by clear and distinct probabilities when discussing questions of natural philosophy on scientific grounds — and it is of these alone that I am at the present moment speaking.

It must be borne in mind distinctly that the discovery of the moon-like phases of Venus, showing her to revolve round the Sun, was simply conclusive as against the old system of Ptolemy, which had so long been the received system of astronomy. The theory of Tycho Brahé, or some modification of it, was the only one that could henceforth be adopted.

But when you dethrone an ancient theory which has for centuries held an almost undisputed sway, you have to reconsider your whole position, and compromises such as that of Tycho are not always adequate to the emergency.

But these considerations formed only a part of this complicated controversy. The anti-Copernicans of the seventeenth century would not even admit the revolution of the Earth on its own axis, and were consequently forced to hold that the whole of the heavenly bodies were carried round this our globe in twenty-four hours. In ancient times, when men knew little or nothing of the sizes and distances of the Sun, the planets, or the stars, such a belief was quite reasonable and natural; they thought the stars were set as if they were jewels in a hollow sphere, which was turned round its poles each day. But the astronomers of Galileo's day knew something far more accurate than this; he himself, as we observed in the Dialogue, greatly under-estimated the distance and the size of the Sun, and had but a very imperfect idea of the enormous interval that separates us from the stars; yet he evidently perceived the improbability of all these vast and remote bodies revolving with an almost inconceivable velocity round the Earth every twenty-four hours. And what must be *our* judgment on such a subject, seeing that we know the Sun's mean distance to be about 92,000,000 miles, more than nineteen times as much as Galileo's estimate? And yet some of the planets are farther and much farther from us than the Sun. Then as regards the stars, α Centauri, the nearest of them, is calculated to be more than 20,000,000,000,000 miles distant; but this calculation supposes the truth of the Copernican theory, and that we may not seem to argue in a circle, we will not use it, but content ourselves with saying that, from certain reasons about which there can be no mistake, we are sure that the distance of the stars is very considerably greater than even the remotest planet in our own system, which is Neptune. Now, this planet's distance from the Sun is computed at 2,775,000,000 miles, and if, indeed, he is carried daily round the Earth in a circle, it must be with a velocity exceeding that of light; the stars, therefore, with a velocity far greater still. Now, nothing with which we are acquainted moves with so great a speed as light—or, as some men call it, *radiant energy,* meaning thereby to include heat as well as light in the term—a speed estimated at 186,000 miles in a second of time. Are we then to believe that the stars are carried in a circle round the Earth every day at a velocity much exceeding even this? It seems almost enough to ask such a question without pausing for the answer. The simple rotation of the Earth on its own axis explains all the phenomena without resorting to such extreme suppositions as those just mentioned.

It is remarkable that no one of any note—at least, in modern times, for I am not so sure about the ancients—ever appears to have suggested the intermediate theory of the Earth revolving on its axis, and yet remaining stationary as regards any motion of translation. With our present knowledge of astronomy we could not entertain such an opinion, though in the early part of the seventeenth century it might have been considered plausible. Since, however, it has not been maintained by any noteworthy author, we need not further discuss it.

The reader will bear in mind what has already been said on this branch of the subject in the second day's dialogue,* and it is not necessary to repeat it in detail. It may, however, be useful to mention a few experiments of a later date, which have tended

---

* I may, perhaps, be permitted to recall to the reader's mind, in a note, one or two of the main objections urged by the anti-Copernicans. One of these was that it would leave the atmosphere behind, the true answer to which is that the atmosphere itself is attracted by the force of gravity to the earth, and is carried round by the rotation, as everything else is; this Galileo did not perfectly understand, as may be seen by his remarks, both in the second and the fourth day's dialogue. Another was this—and it was put forward by no less a man than Tycho Brahé—a stone dropped from a high tower ought to fall to the westward of the tower, because the tower would be carried on to the east by the earth's rotation, and the stone would not; this, however, being contrary to experience. The real fact is that the stone partakes of the rotatory movement as much as the tower does, the two forces of rotation and gravity being combined according to the second law of motion, while the stone is falling; this Galileo did know. Supposing a very high tower, the stone ought to fall slightly to the east, on account of the superior velocity of rotation at the top of the tower to that at the bottom. It is said this experiment has been successfully tried, as stated in note, page 55.

to confirm the truth of the Earth's diurnal revolution.

Before the close of the seventeenth century it was observed that a diminution of gravity occurred at, and near, the equator. This was proved by the vibration of the pendulum, an experiment associated chiefly with the name of Richer; and it has, if I mistake not, been since then carefully tested by spring balances. This phenomenon is owing partly to the spheroidal figure of the Earth,—itself the result of the rotation on the axis—but principally to the centrifugal tendency being greater at the equator, from the higher velocity of rotation.

I have already alluded to the trade winds, and the argument to be drawn from them, which I think a sound and strong one; but I need not dwell on it further.

It is, however, well worth remembering that in our own day another proof has been given, which has been generally allowed to be an important one. It is the result of an experiment of Foucault, and is simply this: if a pendulum, with a heavy weight attached to it, be made to oscillate in a plane due north and south, say in the latitude of Paris, the pendulum, after a time, and supposing it to continue in movement long enough for the purpose of observation, will oscillate in a direction slightly north-east and south-west. Now the pendulum moves naturally always in the same direction, backwards and forwards, as originally started, and if the Earth were shaped like a cylinder no change would be detected; but the spherical form of the Earth, as it rotates on its axis, here makes the whole difference; the floor of the room where the pendulum vibrates is carried round the axis of rotation, as everything else is, but the plane of oscillation remaining the same— or parallel to the original one—it no longer points north and south. At the equator this phenomenon would disappear, and in the southern hemisphere it would be the other way: that is, the pendulum would vibrate north-west and south-east.

The same thing is exemplified by the small machine called the gyroscope, where a heavy disc, so adjusted as to revolve freely in any given direction, independently of the frame in which it is placed, will continue, when once set in rapid motion, to spin in the same plane, directed, for instance, to any one star that happens at the time to be due north or due south of us, while the frame moves round it with the rotation of the Earth.

I think, then, on the whole, we may say that those persons who, in the present state of our knowledge on the subject, are not convinced that the Earth revolves on its own axis, would not be satisfied by any evidence whatever.

Returning now to the general question of Copernicanism, we find that for some time after the trial of Galileo, things remained much *in statu quo;* unless we except the observation of the transit of Venus, in 1639; but, as that eventful seventeenth century was drawing to its close, there came on the scene some thoughtful and able astronomers, who could not only utilise the knowledge of their predecessors, but could also guess, with more or less accuracy, what that law—hitherto unknown—might be, which governed the planets and our own Earth in their movements. It was about this time that the Royal Society was founded in London, and a stimulus was thus given to investigation and to experiment. The third law of Kepler, which states that in all the planetary orbits the square of the periodic time of revolution is in a constant proportion to the cube of the mean distance, suggested the existence of another law, not yet discovered, a law of attraction, on which this itself depended. Among the astronomers of that day three names deserve special mention, Wren, Hooke, and Halley, because each of them guessed with some accuracy at the true doctrine — as it is now known to be — that the planets are attracted to the Sun by a force which acts inversely as the square of the distance. Hooke, in particular, deserves the credit of having applied this law to the path of a projectile, under certain circumstances, as well as to the planetary orbits; but though he thus lighted upon true conclusions, he appears to have been deficient in mathematical skill, and therefore unable to verify his results. It is, however, only just to the memory of Horrox, who was carried off by an early death, to mention that the true theory of the identity of terrestrial and astronomical gravity had occurred to his mind; if he had lived twenty or thirty years longer, he might have survived in history as the discoverer of the great problem.

Be this as it may, there now arose another man greater than his predecessors, and greater than all his contemporaries; he also was an Englishman, by name Isaac Newton. What others guessed, or concluded on insufficient evidence, became, in his powerful hands, clear and well-grounded truths, proved, so far as such things could be proved, by rigid mathematical reasoning, and established on a solid basis, which time has not shaken, and which subsequent investigation has confirmed. Others had supposed the existence of the law of attraction by which the Sun acted on the planets; many persons had understood the existence of terrestrial gravitation. Newton showed that these two are identical; and, moreover, that every particle of matter attracts every other particle *mutually*, and according to the one universal law, that of the inverse square of the distance; so that a vast planet revolving round the Sun obeys the same law as a pebble dropped from one's hand to the Earth. The popular story of his having been suddenly led to this conclusion by the sight of an apple falling is apparently fabulous; and what really occurred is this: he sat alone one day in a garden, and fell into a speculation (as men of scientific mind are apt to do) on the power of gravity, that is, of gravity as we feel it here on the Earth. Then it struck him that however high you ascend, even on the loftiest mountains, no sensible diminution in this remarkable force takes place; so, he said to himself: why not as high as the Moon? If so, perhaps she is retained in her orbit by this very power. And again if so, what then? To which question his active mind gave the just and true answer, that it was probably one and the same force that acted at the surface of the Earth, at the distance of the Moon, and finally, as regulating the action of the Sun on the planets.

It seems that there was an error, which it is unnecessary to explain in detail, in Newton's first calculations; but that when, after a lapse of time and with the error corrected, he again returned to them, he found the motion of the Moon to be exactly accounted for by his theory.

Again, in dealing with the complicated problem of the action of the heavenly bodies one upon the other, that is, when the disturbing force, for instance, of a third body is brought to bear on the motions of two others, although Hooke and others had as a conjecture put forth the existence of such mutual action, yet Newton was the first who thoroughly grappled with it.

The mutual attraction of matter, so far as things terrestrial are concerned, had occurred to the inquiring intellect of Francis Bacon; but it was left for Newton to propound it as the great principle that governs the physical universe.

Now let us see how all this bears on the truth of the Copernican system. Newton proved—and I may add that the improved methods of mathematics which have been adopted since his day make the proofs more simple and easy—that if any body moves in an ellipse, or indeed, in one of the other conic sections, the law of force, tending to the focus, is that of the inverse square of the distance.* Conversely, he proved that a body under the action of a central force, varying in intensity as the inverse square of the distance, will move in a conic section.

Then if the Moon moved in an ellipse, as it was easy to perceive that she did, and if her motion corresponded precisely with what it would be on the theory of universal gravitation; if also, as seemed evident, the planets revolved in ellipses, then the inference that the law of gravitation, as stated by Newton, was true became irresistible; not susceptible, as before stated, of direct and absolute proof, but established conclusively by a sound and legitimate induction.

* There are other laws, besides that of the inverse square of the distance, which would cause a body to move in an ellipse, at least if the force acting on it were placed, not in the focus, but in the centre of the orbit. The question has been discussed with reference to some of the binary stars which appear to move round one another in ellipses. No doubt is thereby raised as to the prevalence of the law of the inverse square in our own solar system, where it has been verified by long and careful observation; the doubt (I think we may say a comparatively slight one) is whether the same law extends to the whole stellar universe, where, of course, accurate observation is impracticable.

What I have just stated shows that Kepler's first law corresponds with Newton's discovery; but the same is true of the two other laws. It would of course be out of place here to go minutely into all the evidence which can be gathered in support of the doctrine of universal gravitation. I may briefly state that all of Kepler's laws are simply explicable by that hypothesis, and that the evidence derives additional confirmation from the following curious fact: observation shows that Kepler's laws, though approximately true, are not strictly and accurately so; if the planets were mere particles revolving round the Sun, they would then be quite rigidly true, but the planets have a certain mass (though very small compared to the Sun) and so do in some measure attract the Sun as well as being attracted by him, and they, moreover, exercise a disturbing influence on each other. These perturbations, however, have been calculated, and the result is that they agree with what ought reasonably to be expected, supposing the theory of universal gravitation to be true. This confirmatory proof has been acquired, I need not add, since the time of Newton by the labours of astronomers, Laplace and others, who have succeeded him, and who have had the advantage of that more manageable method of mathematical calculation to which I have just alluded.

Supposing then the law of gravitation to be established by sufficient proof, we may now ask what must become of the old systems of astronomy? What must befall Ptolemy and even Tycho Brahé?

It is obvious that they could do nothing but collapse. If the law of gravitation were once admitted to be true, the idea of the Sun revolving round the Earth must be dismissed as impossible. Here it is right to remark that (assuming the law of universal gravitation) it is not, strictly and scientifically speaking, correct to say that any one heavenly body revolves round another, but that they both revolve round their common centre of gravity. In the case of the Earth and the Sun, so vastly superior is the mass of the latter that the centre of gravity is far away within his volume, and the disturbance exercised on him by the Earth is scarcely appreciable; so also, in the case of the Moon and the Earth, the centre of gravity is within the latter, but at a considerable distance from its own centre; and here there is a distinctly appreciable oscillation of the Earth, arising from this very cause, during each revolution of the Moon in her orbit. When two bodies are more nearly equal in mass, as is probably the case with the double stars that have been observed in recent times, then the two revolve round a centre of gravity lying between them, exterior to both of them. It is believed that this is actually the fact in the instance I am here alluding to of the double stars, and there is some reason for supposing that the curve in which they revolve is an ellipse. This, if true, would clearly indicate that the law of gravitation, as stated by

Newton, extends not only through our own solar system, but over the whole material universe.

And there is one remarkable property of this mysterious agency which we term gravitation, and that is its instantaneous action even at the greatest distances. Light travels with an enormous and yet a finite velocity, so that it takes a few years to arrive at the Earth from even the nearest stars. The force of gravity knows no such limit, nor is its action retarded by even the minutest fraction of time.

Nor, again, is it impeded, as in the case of light, by any screen or obstacle of whatever nature. Furthermore, it does not lose anything of its intensity, as light does, by being diffused over a larger surface; it varies as the *mass* of the bodies concerned, but not in the least according to the extent of their surfaces. Given the same distance, no diffusion weakens its force.

Great as was the evidence adduced by Newton for the truth of his theory, there were some real difficulties in the way of its reception. I need not allude to these in detail; they are explained in treatises on physical astronomy for the benefit of those who are interested in the subject. Briefly, I may say that subsequent research and careful calculations have removed the difficulties, and thereby confirmed the already existing evidence.

Then, as regards terrestrial gravity, experiments have been made—notably at the mountain Schehallion, in Scotland—throwing additional light upon it, and indicating that not merely the Earth as a whole, but any great mass, such as a mountain, exercises an appreciable attractive force.

Newton seems to have expected that some further discovery would take place, at no distant period, as to the nature of this occult agency which operates so powerfully in the heavens and on the Earth. In one of his letters he strongly disclaims the opinion that gravity is essential to matter and inherent in it; he thinks it is "inconceivable that inanimate brute matter should, without the mediation of something else which is not material, operate on and affect other matter without mutual contact . . . . that gravity should be innate, inherent, and essential to matter, so that one body may act upon another at a distance through a *vacuum*, without the mediation of anything else by and through which their action and force may be conveyed from one to another, is to me so great an absurdity that I believe no man who has in philosophical matters a competent faculty of thinking can ever fall into it."

And yet we see that what he thought absurd is still apparently true, and that, great as was Newton's sagacity in discovering and proving the effects of this great cosmical law, he failed when he came to speculate on the more remote causes of it. Since his time, other ingenious theorists have imagined hypotheses in the hopes of accounting for it; but their efforts have not met with any great success, and the last word of science on the subject is that the cause of gravitation remains undiscovered.

But if the attempt to trace the ultimate cause of the law of gravitation has been a failure, the proof of its operation in the physical universe has been a marvellous success, and that not only in the present day, when difficulties have been removed and fresh evidence has been added, but, to a certain extent, even in Newton's own time, and especially here in his own country. Indeed, we cannot suppress a feeling of admiration when we contemplate the revolution in astronomy brought about by this quiet, unobtrusive man, who is said to have spent thirty-five years of his long life within the walls of Trinity College, Cambridge, of which he was a Fellow, and who, though twice elected to represent the University in Parliament, never opened his lips in the House of Commons. I may, perhaps, be here permitted to insert a passage from a work to which I have previously alluded, Whewell's "History of the Inductive Sciences," well worth quoting both for its eloquence and its truth. After recounting, with some detail, the circumstances of this great epoch in astronomical knowledge, he proceeds :

> Such, then, is the great Newtonian induction of universal gravitation, and such its history. It is indisputably and incomparably the greatest scientific discovery ever made, whether we look at the advance which it involved, the extent of the truth disclosed, or the fundamental and satisfactory nature of this truth. As to the first point, we may observe that any one of the five steps

into which we have separated the doctrine [these were, 1st, that the force attracting *different* planets to the sun, and, 2nd, the force attracting the *same* planet in different parts of its orbit, is as the inverse square of the distances; 3rd, that the earth exerts such a force on the moon, and that this is identical with terrestrial gravity; 4th, that there is a *mutual* attraction of the heavenly bodies on one another; 5th, that there exists a mutual attraction of *all particles of matter* throughout the universe] would of itself have been considered as an important advance, would have conferred distinction on the persons who made it, and the time to which it belonged. All the five steps made at once formed not a leap, but a flight; not an improvement merely, but a metamorphosis; not an epoch, but a termination. Astronomy passed at once from its boyhood to mature manhood. Again, with regard to the extent of the truth, we obtain as wide a generalisation as our physical knowledge admits when we learn that every particle of matter, in all times, places, and circumstances, attracts every other particle in the universe by one common law of action. And by saying that the truth was of a fundamental and satisfactory nature, I mean that it assigned, not a rule merely, but a cause, for the heavenly motions; and that kind of cause which most eminently and peculiarly we distinctly and thoroughly conceive, namely, mechanical force. Kepler's laws were merely *formal* rules, governing the celestial motions according to the relations of space, time, and number; Newton's was a *causal* law, referring these motions to mechanical reasons. It is no doubt conceivable that future discoveries may both extend and further explain Newton's doctrines; may make gravitation a case of some wider law, and may disclose something of the way in which it operates—questions with which Newton himself struggled. But, in the meantime, few persons will dispute that, both in generality and profundity, both in width and depth, Newton's theory is without a rival or neighbour.[*]

The effect of all this on the Copernican system and the evidence on which it rested, was to raise that

[*] I do not think the truth of this is affected by any of the great modern discoveries; though that of the Conservation of Energy approaches more nearly than others to Universal Gravitation in its importance.

system from a simple though strong probability, a question on which at any rate something might be said for and against it, to a probability of almost overwhelming force; for it not only showed how the heavenly bodies moved, but it explained the cause of their motions, and in a word furnished the key that unlocked the arcana of Nature. When you came to know not only how the Moon and the planets moved, but the law which regulated their movements, and when you found that all fitted into one harmonious whole (at least with some minor exceptions), it was not easy to refuse assent to a theory supported by such powerful evidence.

Yet in saying this we are perhaps rather viewing the question from our present standpoint, than as a contemporary would have done. As a matter of fact, Newton's hypothesis, though eagerly received in England, met with a long opposition on the Continent, and particularly in France, where Descartes' theory of vortices reigned supreme for many years. It must not be supposed that these Cartesian philosophers were anti-Copernicans; far otherwise, only they accounted for the celestial motions in a different way from Newton, and, as every one now admits, in a wrong way.

I have already remarked that there were some apparent difficulties in the application of the law of universal gravitation to all the heavenly bodies, and that these have been removed by subsequent calculation. One of these difficulties, if indeed it could be so called (for it hardly amounted to that), has been solved within living memory. It was noticed that the planet Uranus showed signs of perturbation from some unknown reason; and even the work I have just quoted, "Whewell's History of the Inductive Sciences," published in 1847, contains the following sentence: "Uranus still deviates from his tabular place, and the cause remains yet to be discovered." Two astronomers, one French and one English, Le Verrier and Adams, found out the cause by discovering the existence, each independently of the other, of an exterior planet revolving in an orbit more distant by far than that of Uranus; to this planet the name of Neptune has been given, and his existence is one more confirmatory proof of the theory of gravitation.

The Copernican system had been built up and consolidated by Newton's great discovery; but another piece of evidence, of a most important character, was added by the investigations of Bradley, Professor of Astronomy at Oxford, and afterwards Astronomer Royal; this careful observer, while engaged in endeavouring to detect such an apparent motion of the fixed stars (so called) as would indicate an annual parallax, noticed that another motion existed different from that which the annual parallax would produce, and for which he could not account; the apparent orbits described by the stars observed depended on the distance of the stars from the pole of the ecliptic; the phenomenon was different from anything hitherto discovered, and one or two modes of explanation were tried in vain. Accident, however, turned Bradley's thoughts in the right direction; he was one day in a boat on the Thames, and observed that the vane on the mast gave a different apparent direction to the wind, according as the boat sailed in different courses. Here, then, was the solution of the difficulty: it was already known from Römer's investigations that light moved with a finite velocity, and if so it would naturally produce the same effect as that observed in the boat, or to take an illustration very commonly given, like that which any one finds when moving along rapidly in a shower of rain, in which latter case the rain seems to fall not in the direction it has when one is at rest, but in a direction compounded of that and the one opposite to the person's line of motion.

Bradley soon drew the correct conclusion, that light acted in precisely the same way upon the Earth as it moved in its orbit, and that the *apparent* annual displacement of the stars, as detected by him, arose from this sole cause. All the great astronomers who followed him have agreed with his conclusions, and the phenomenon in question, which is called the aberration of light, has conferred a lasting fame on its discoverer. And the remarkable point about it is this, that not only does it give a fresh illustration to the Copernican theory, but it is one of the very few scientific facts that cannot (so far as our knowledge of the subject goes) be explained in any other way.

It is, therefore, generally considered as a critical test of the truth of the system.

There are two other phenomena, on which however I do not propose to dwell at any length, known as precession and nutation, which it is not easy to explain otherwise than by the modern theory of astronomy and the principle of gravitation; the latter of these two owed its discovery to Bradley, and the former to Hipparchus, who could not have been aware of its real cause, though he had observed the fact of its occurrence.

But passing on from these, I may call attention to one most remarkable result of modern scientific research, connected with the stars. In Galileo's day, it was a drawback to the Copernican theory that none of the stars showed the smallest annual parallax; in popular language, none of them seemed to undergo any change of place, however small, when observed at opposite points of the Earth's orbit, or as the opponents would have said, the Earth's imagined orbit. A displacement of this kind, I need hardly repeat, must not be confounded with that other motion which Bradley observed and explained. This was one of Tycho Brahé's reasons for rejecting the Copernican system, and it was one of the best arguments used by the opponents of Galileo. As the enormous distance of the stars from the Earth was, as we have already seen, at that time unknown, the celestial distances generally being under-estimated even by the best astronomers, the argument had an apparent force, which no one now would attribute to it. Galileo himself had some hope of overcoming the difficulty by discovering some annual displacement in certain stars, but it is needless to add that his instruments were unequal to such a task. Subsequent observers tried various methods, but without any real success until the present century, when Bessel and other observers found that a star called 61 Cygni had a certain annual parallax; and not long afterwards, Henderson, making his observations at the Cape of Good Hope on a conspicuous star in the constellation of the Centaur, a constellation belonging to the southern hemisphere, found at length that this star, which in fact is a double star, and known as α Centauri, had a parallax of nearly $1''$; subsequent calculations show it to be probably rather less, that is to say about $0''\cdot 91$. This means that it is more than twenty billions of miles distant, and that light takes more than three years to travel from α Centauri to the earth. It is, however, believed to be much the nearest of all the stars, no other coming within double of the distance.

Now it is difficult to evade the conclusion which naturally follows from these results, that the Earth really does move in an annual orbit round the Sun. It is no part of my present task to give a list of the stars of which the parallax has been found, but I may say there are several others besides the two I have named; and I know of no method of accounting for the fact in any way but by the annual motion of the Earth, unless we suppose some instrumental error to have occurred. There have been so many of these in times past that it may seem rash to exclude such a possibility, but, considering the perfection of modern scientific instruments, it is in the highest degree improbable; and we may fairly reckon the parallaxes of the stars as a strong confirmation of the already strong evidence in favour of the Copernican theory—a theory which, as we have seen, was, from a purely scientific point of view, very probable in the days of Galileo, overwhelmingly probable after the great discovery of Newton, and at the present time, with all the light that subsequent research and observation have thrown on it, scarcely short of a moral certainty.

I may repeat once more that it has not, indeed, that absolute physical certainty, arising from direct experiment, which has been obtained in other scientific investigations; but, allowing for this faint element of instability, we may fairly say that no truth of natural philosophy stands on a firmer basis.

And for Galileo, who lived before the day when, as Whewell says, "Astronomy passed from boyhood to mature manhood," we may fairly say that, after we have censured his faults and his errors, after we have ascertained that he was not a hero or a "martyr of science," we must still recognise the fact that he was one of the greatest natural philosophers of his day, pre-eminent in astronomy, in mechanics, in mathematics. To his honour also be it added, that his religious faith, and his respect for the Church and her authority, so far as we can judge, never failed. Whatever his defects may have been—want of prudence, want of candour, want of consideration for others—we can easily perceive that he would never have been willingly drawn into any controversy intended to provoke antagonism between Religion and Science.

In the present age, unhappily, there have been men who have taken the other course, and have contributed their share towards exciting antagonism, heedless of the consequences. Some have done this unwittingly, arguing on the side of religion, but without a proper supply of sound scientific information; others, on the opposite side, have shown so bitterly hostile a spirit to Revelation, if not even to Natural Religion, as to render it more than ever difficult to re-establish that concord between the two studies, that of the supernatural and that of the physical, which should never have been interrupted.

This, however, is so wide a subject that I must not be led into it. Yet I may briefly remark that two of the greatest lights of the Catholic Church, men whose teaching and whose writings have exercised an undying influence, have both, either by words explicitly, or implicitly by their example, contributed to encourage a sound knowledge of natural philosophy, and in harmony with Christian theology.

They both lived when physical science was in its infancy, though at intervals of nearly 800 years apart. St. Augustine, who flourished towards the latter part of that period dominated by the corrupt civilisation of ancient Rome, amongst his voluminous works devoted one treatise to the interpretation of the Book of Genesis, "De Genesi ad Litteram;" and he takes the opportunity of cautioning those whom he addresses against the risk of exciting the ridicule of unbelievers by a mistaken adherence to a rigidly literal interpretation of Holy Scripture. He was, I believe, one of the first that interpreted the six days of Creation in the non-literal sense, though his particular theory is not one in accordance with modern scientific opinion. I allude to him not for the details of natural philosophy, but as enunciating a principle, which some subsequent authors have not followed as they might have done.

St. Thomas Aquinas lived in those middle ages of which he was one of the most brilliant ornaments. The power of his intellect is admitted by those who have little sympathy with his teaching; his literary industry is a standing marvel; and I have already observed that besides the theological and metaphysical works on which he expended so much labour, he wrote a treatise on the astronomy of Aristotle. It may be said this is no very great matter, but I mention it as illustrating the breadth of mind of this great saint and theologian, who could spare time for a study of physical science without neglecting the more solemn duties of his calling. His active mind was alive to every source from whence wisdom and learning could be imbibed; and if he had lived in the age of Galileo, I have sometimes fancied that he would have thrown some oil on the troubled waters, would have counselled prudence to the adventurous astronomer, patience and forbearance to his antagonists. But it is of no avail to indulge in speculations such as these. Each age of the world has its difficulties, moral and intellectual, and we can neither hurry the stream of human thought onwards nor drive it backwards.

So again it is with the dispositions of individuals; if Galileo had been gifted with the calm, dignified reserve of Newton, instead of being the vivacious, loquacious Italian that he in fact was, he might have lived and died in peace.

And now, if I may be permitted to recur once more to the subject of gravitation, I have a word to say as to the lesson which this great all-pervading law seems to teach. It has nothing to do with any question of revealed Religion; but does it not bear the unmistakable signs of the action of an all-wise, an all-powerful Creator? It may possibly be the result of some other, though unknown, law; and even then it brings us back to the same point. The result in nature remains the same, and that result is written in characters that cannot be ignored. Mathematicians have occupied themselves in making suppositions as to the effects of imaginary laws of gravity, some of which might, no doubt, ensure sufficient order and regularity to maintain this world, and the countless worlds that people space, while others would cause hopeless confusion. The striking thing is that the existing law perfectly answers its purpose.

Only let us imagine that no law of attraction acted upon matter at all, nor any force of whatever kind— what would be the result? There would be no coherence, no abode for human or animal life— nothing but chaos and anarchy.

If, then, we contrast this imagined picture with the one actually before us, we are, I think, forcibly led to the conclusion that the physical universe owes its origin, its existence, its harmony to an Omnipotent Being, unseen, yet not unknown, intangible to the senses, ever present to the intelligence.

And now, in order to avoid misapprehension, I venture to restate briefly the propositions I have sought to establish.

I have maintained that the Catholic Church has a right to lay her restraining hand on the speculations of Natural Science, just as much as she has in the case of other speculative inquiries. Those who do not believe in her prerogatives will, of course, deny such right *in toto*; but I contend that if you grant the existence of this right at all, you cannot exclude Physical Science from its operation.

On the other hand, in the particular case of Galileo, I have not attempted to defend all the proceedings of the Cardinals of the Index and the Cardinals of the Inquisition. For it must be remembered it was no gentle rebuke with which the Copernican system and the individual Galileo were visited; no such light condemnation as that of placing on the Index of prohibited books all Copernican works as being *inopportune*, or again, that of a caution to Galileo to be more prudent, was deemed adequate to the emergency—if, indeed, any one even thought of them.

So with the facts of the history before us, I think any sweeping defence of the proceedings in question would be unnecessary from an ecclesiastical point of view, and from a scientific point of view untenable.

Moreover, I must add, as an indispensable premiss to the conclusion just stated, I have also maintained that the censures pronounced by the Cardinals on both occasions were not dogmatic decisions, such as Catholic theologians hold to be infallible; but disciplinary enactments, varying with the changing characters of different ages.

Then again, referring to the scientific questions involved, we may see that Astronomy, considered historically, is divided into three periods—the ancient one before the invention of the telescope, that is, up to the time of Galileo; the intermediate one, when the telescope was in use but the law of universal gravitation as yet unknown—from Galileo until the publication of the "Principia" of Newton; and the modern one, from Newton downwards. During the first period it seemed highly probable to the whole world, with the exception of a few gifted intellects, that this Earth was the centre of the Universe, and that all the heavenly bodies revolved round it; during the second period, when the telescope had shed a light so powerful and so brilliant upon astronomical research that men could not absolutely close their eyes to it even if they wished, the balance of probability passed into the opposite scale, and the more intelligent men of science guessed at the truth, however indistinctly. But some elements of uncertainty remained; and this circumstance, taken in connection with the irrelevant arguments so much in vogue at that time, must in all fairness be allowed as an excuse for the many good men, ecclesiastics and others, who opposed the Copernican doctrine. After the great step made by Newton it was no longer a question of balancing probabilities, for the weights were almost all transferred to one scale, and the probabilities of the truth of the Heliocentric System (to give it for once its accurate name) became overwhelming. The subsequent investigations of Bradley and others have gone further still, and have converted this strong, overpowering probability into something approaching indefinitely near to a moral certainty.

Beyond this we cannot reasonably expect to go; *physical* certainty is not to be attained when we have to traverse the vast distances of celestial space, and human infirmity must be content to recognise the boundary beyond which it may not pass, the limit imposed on finite minds by the Infinite.

THE END.